INNOVATIVE THEORY AND PRACTICE OF BADMINTON

March L. Krotee
University of Minnesota

Edward T. Turner
Appalachian State University

**KENDALL/HUNT
PUBLISHING COMPANY**
Dubuque, Iowa

B   403152   01

Contents

Foreword

This text presents the fundamentals of the game of Badminton, and the basics of how to play it, in a way that should enforce its practical value. In a way, Badminton is unique, in that it can be enjoyed at all levels of play, from the free-wheeling casualness of outdoor play in a backyard or park to the disciplined complexity of international competition outdoors—and the authors have spelled out the patterns of practice and play that can help to develop the skills of players who want to raise their standards of performance.

Good badminton play is far more complex than is realized by many people who have never seen the game played well. So, patience and thoroughness in following the instructions set out in this text are essential to raising one's level of skills.

Excellent as this book is in its presentation of the patterns to be followed, a greater challenge to many participants in the game will be to find the facilities in which to practice, and allocate time to carry out the recommended drills. As in any other human activity, success in using the practice patterns will depend upon the commitment of the individual to improve.

Edwin S. Jarrett
Vice President
International Badminton Federation

Preface

After two decades of primary involvement in the game of badminton as both competitors and instructors, we have recognized a lucid need for an innovative approach to the tremendous and challenging game of badminton. Most texts, however, seem to offer only superficial approaches to the game henceforth the motivation for our text.

The text, although far from a complete probe into this most traditional of racquet sports, is designed in a manageable and meaningful fashion so the reader can enjoy, learn, appreciate and explore the complex world of badminton. Chapter 1 provides the reader with an insight into the roots and nature of the game. Chapter 2 describes the preparation the participant should undergo in order to be ready to play. Chapters 3 through 10 elucidate the skill involvement in playing as well as offering creative tips and "thought provokers" for the reader. Chapter 11 provides suggestions for improvement in various dimensions of the game while Chapter 12 describes the equipment and facilities requisite for play. Chapters 13 and 14 present the Laws of Badminton as well as the sports terminology. The text concludes with a reference guide for literature and teaching aids as well as suggested creative activities for the game. We sincerely hope you enjoy the text, but more crucial, we hope you enjoy a long and pleasant association with the great game of badminton.

March L. Krotee
Edward T. Turner

Acknowledgments

The authors are indepted to and wish to express sincere gratitude to Edwin S. Jarrett, Vice President of the International Badminton Federation for his guidance concerning the content of this text. We also wish to thank Patty Beckmann, Pennie Krotee Grimes and Geri Valind for their care and thoroughness in the preparation of this manuscript. The first author wishes to express a special thanks to Leslie, Chip and Rob for providing the necessary support to undertake such a time consuming endeavor, and the second author would like to acknowledge and thank Luke and Matt for their sincere interest in sports and their support in helping their father complete this effort.

March L. Krotee
Edward T. Turner

The Game

Introduction and Brief History

Some historians believe that an early form of badminton known as battledore or shuttlecock was played more than two thousand years ago in China and Siam. Other researchers have traced various forms of badminton to 12th Century England and 17th Century Poland. Today, however, most researchers and badminton enthusiasts tend to agree that badminton has its more modern roots in a game known as poona which was derived from the town of Poona, India, where an early form of the game apparently flourished. This mystical form of badminton was then transmitted to England by English army officers in the early 1870's. In 1873 the game was introduced at the Duke of Beaufort's summer home of "Badminton" in Gloucestershire, England, where the game received its now internationally recognized name of badminton and the sport gained in popularity.

In 1895 the Badminton Association of England was instituted and in 1902 European countries began to host international competitions. In 1934 the International Badminton Federation was founded with Canada, Denmark, England, France, Ireland, Netherlands, New Zealand, Scotland and Wales as the founder nations. Today, several Asian countries, including India, Indonesia, Malaysia and Thailand, recognize badminton as their national sport and indeed, these countries and Japan have grasped total domination of all men's International Badminton Championships since the championships were inaugurated in 1948.

Badminton first came to the United States in 1878 at the 71st Regiment Armory Club in New York City and slowly spread as a fashionable sport through some of the more exclusive private clubs in major Eastern urban settings. The original rules of the game were standardized in 1877, revised in 1887 and 1890 and for the most part remain intact today. The growth of badminton was slow and remained relatively confined through the 1920's and 1930's. During this era many individuals received their first view of badminton as a stage show that was part of the vaudeville circuit which included acts featuring badminton demonstrations by touring English and Canadian professionals. These professionals usually traveled the vaudeville circuit as well as playing the small racquet clubs of the immediate area in order to spark interest in the sport of badminton. The state of badminton at this particular point in time was that it was very popular in England, quite wide spread throughout the Canadian provinces, with the Canadian Badminton Association beginning in 1930, gaining in global recognition with the establishment of the International Badminton Federation (IBF) in 1934, but still comparatively dormant in the United States. In 1936, under the leadership of Bostonian Donald Wilbur, sixty-five clubs banded together to form the American Badminton Association, which became an affiliate of the International Badminton Federation in 1937. That same year the inaugural United States tournament for amateurs was held in Chicago and badminton had realized a new image. The days of the touring professional badminton player expired together with the stage show era of vaudeville and with the exception of the USO professional touring circuit during World War II, badminton was no longer presented before the American public in this professional stage form. Indeed, even the private racquet clubs began to fade in popularity and were forced to alter their emphasis in favor of other racket sports such as squash and tennis.

World War II seriously lead to the demise and diminishment of most sports and badminton was no exception. After the war, however, a fresh surge of interest in badminton lead to the start of organized, worldwide competition and the institution of the Cup competitions for men's and women's teams signified the rebirth of the game. The 1948–49 season saw the beginning of play for the Thomas Cup, a handsome silver trophy donated by Sir George Thomas, a great player and Founder-President of the IBF, emblematic of the World's Men's Team Championship. Subsequently, during the 1956–57 season, competition began for the Uber Cup, donated by Mrs. Betty Uber, one of England's all-time great players, which was awarded for the World Women's Team Championship. Since these beginnings, except for the first three Uber Cup competitions which were won by the United States, these two trophies have been continuously in the hands of Asiatic countries, i.e., Malaya (now Malaysia), Indonesia, Japan and China where badminton is truly a major, and almost the national sport.

The two Cup competitions have, up to now, been held every third year—on a 'staggered' basis, and each 'tie' has consisted of 9 matches (5 singles and 4 doubles). The world-wide play was divided into 4 geographical zones, with the respective zone winners assembling for a 'play-down' to determine the champion. The total format has recently been changed to provide that the two Cup competitions will now be conducted simultaneously every other year (in seasons ending in an even-numbered year), in alternation with the World Championships tournaments, and each Cup 'tie' will consist of only 5 matches (3 singles and 2 doubles). These changes were instituted to stimulate greater participation as well as to reduce the overall costs and management difficulties in the administration of such a world class event.

Today the resurgence of first class badminton is coming through the schools, colleges, and universities and particularly through the growth of intercollegiate competition. Over a decade ago the Life Time Sports Education Project, in conjunction with the National Education Association, the American Badminton Association and the American Alliance for Health, Physical Education, Recreation and Dance started regional programs to introduce badminton into school programs across the nation. The results of that project are now beginning to be evidenced by the caliber of play exhibited by students in tournaments at the collegiate, national, and international levels.

The American Badminton Association, which for over 40 years was organized primarily by clubs, has now restructured it organizational pattern to include individual and institutional memberships, which has generated a new population of interested participants. To keep pace with this restructuring, the American Badminton Association has altered its name to the United States Badminton Association. The popularity that badminton is now enjoying resides in a renaissance of the involved participant. The average citizen and student recognizes badminton as a sociable, easily learned, and highly enjoyable recreative game but also recognizes its inherent value to the total maintenance of health and physical fitness. The modern era of badminton has arrived. The future of the sport as well as the physiological and psychosocial benefit to the individual participant seem to reflect and project a bright future for the game of badminton.

The Nature and Future of the Game

Badminton is a racket and net game played by either two (singles), one on a side, or four (doubles) players, two on a side. The object of the game is to propel the shuttlecock over the five foot (1.524 meter) net, five feet one inch (1.55 meters) at the posts, into the opponent's side of the court in such a manner that the opposition cannot return the shuttlecock. Play continues until one side reaches 15 points in the case of men's games or 11 points in the case of women's games. A side may only score a point when serving and a match consists of the best two of three games.

Badminton is a lifetime sport that can be played both indoors and outdoors. Badminton has been characterized as the game with the widest variation of implement speed in sport. The shuttlecock is believed to be one of the slowest implements in sport, yet speeds in excess of 100 MPH or 160 km/hr can be obtained during a smash shot.

Because of the light weight racket, 3.5–5.0 oz. (99.23–141gms) and shuttle (73–85 grains), the game of badminton is relatively easy for the beginner to obtain some degree of immediate skill and success. Because of this success or satisfaction factor combined with the game's physiological suitability for all age groups, badminton has been classified as a lifetime sport. The sport is an ideal game for the young child as well as the older participant as badminton seems to possess a uniqueness that enables its characteristics and values to adapt to the participant's age, level of skill and degree of competitiveness. Badminton is a highly social, pleasurable, recreative experience which can be enjoyed and participated in throughout life. Badminton, however, may also offer to the most intense competitor as much physiological and psychological challenge that exists in any sport. The sport of badminton and the pace and competitive intensity with which individuals may wish to participate seem to be as significant in variability as the speed of the flight of the shuttle. Badminton is truly a game for all seasons, ages and levels of expertise and experience.

As with many recreative dual and individual sports, the future of the game of badminton may be subject to various rule changes, new scoring techniques, and technological changes in equipment. It is obvious that many of these have already taken place or are in the process of development and will continue to evolve. These technical and technological advances together with the development of new strokes and new basic mechanical stroke technique will improve the game for both the participant and for the spectator insuring a bright and active transnational future for the game.

Thought Provoker

Look closely at the following and attempt to find as many terms, items, and other meaningful tidbits that are related to the game of badminton.

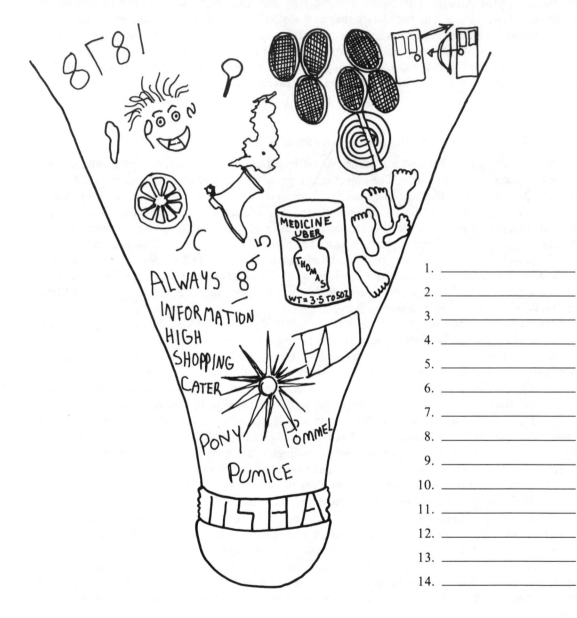

1. _____
2. _____
3. _____
4. _____
5. _____
6. _____
7. _____
8. _____
9. _____
10. _____
11. _____
12. _____
13. _____
14. _____

Check Appendix A to identify the correct answers. The number of correct responses places you in the following category.

Correct Answers		Category
9	=	Novice
10	=	Average
11	=	Above Average
12	=	Expert
13	=	Professional
14	=	"Bashing" Job!
15	=	"Smashing"

Pre-Game Preparation

Physical and Mental
Creative Tips
Thought Provoker

2

Physical and Mental

There seems to be a great deal of controversy as to the actual benefits of warm-up activity. It is generally agreed upon, however, that warm-up is an individual matter with some participants needing very little warm-up and others needing to work quite intensely to prepare themselves. In an official badminton match, pre-game warm-up is usually limited to three to five minutes or left to the discretion of the umpire. The warm-up usually takes place by rallying with the opponent. It is recommended that the player engage in ten to fifteen minutes of warm-up before participating in a strenuous match. During this time period a five minute recovery or tapering off period should be employed just before beginning play.

The warm-up should be intense enough to increase the heart rate, blood pressure and body temperature but should not cause undue fatigue. The warm-up should include general stretching and loosening exercises as well as specific movement pattern practice in order to prepare specific muscle groups for the precision like tasks that lie ahead. These specific movement patterns should include the player's complement of badminton shots. These shots should be practiced until some degree of both physiological and psychological readiness is reached and the player feels and believes that he or she as well as the opponent is ready to perform to his or her maximal potential. Normally, the opponent will complement your warm-up by "setting" the shuttle to you in order for you to practice your full repertoire of badminton shots.

The physiological value of warm-up is to 1) increase the speed and force of the muscle contraction, 2) improve coordination and timing, 3) help prevent injuries to muscles, tendons and ligaments and 4) assist in the mobilization of the body's resources for action. Another value of warm-up is to mentally prepare the player for the pending competition. The player should be mentally preparing for the competition, mentally rehearsing particular movement patterns and concentrating on the game strategy. This mental preparation serves to activate the player's nervous and endocrine systems and may indirectly affect other physiological functions stimulated and controlled by the sympathetic nervous system. During any warm-up, primary consideration should be given to the legs (footwork), trunk and back area (light static stretching) and dominant arm and wrist areas (practicing stroke skill technique patterns) since these are the major physical parameters that are stressed during badminton competition.

Another value of the pre-game preparation period is that it enables the player to study the game conditions and immediate court environment. Variables such as equipment, lighting, court surface texture and other factors such as ceiling clearance and general court distractions should be explored. If possible, the opponent should be studied during the warm-up period as to possible strengths and weaknesses which may be incorporated into your game plan. Specific items in regard to the opponent's movement patterns should also be gleaned in order to determine the types, speed and strength of his or her repertoire of game skills, particularly the opponent's repertoire of backhand shots. In effect, the warm-up period allows the player to become aware and mentally prepared for the match. The importance of mental preparation may be a crucial factor in a match and should not be taken for granted.

In summary, the pre-game preparation or warm-up period should be used to physically and mentally prepare the player in order to meet the specific goals that have been set for the match. These goals may vary in range from winning a championship competition to getting a vigorous and recreative work out. This variation in goal expectancy is one of the tremendous advantages about participation in badminton over other types of group activities.

Creative Tips

Attempt to take 5–10 minutes of mental rehearsal warm-up in solitude with no physical warm-up. Some research has indicated that concentrated visualization or mental imagery of various well-learned skills has had a positive effect on skill performance. Take each stroke and picture or visualize the mechanical aspects of the stroke including the feeling of the ultimate winning of the point. Think of proper stroke movement patterns as well as the physiological and skill or technique advantages you have over your opponent.

Warm-up for recreational play with oversized rackets, undersized rackets, flexible rackets, stiff rackets, various size and shaped shuttles, textured balls or other foreign objects. Try mini-badminton on a smaller court, restricted area badminton, or badminton with two rackets per player. Take a different as well as varied look at the basic game strokes and equipment. It will add a new dimension as well as added enjoyment to your warm-up regime.

Figure 2.1. Mental practice.

Thought Provoker

Complete the following crossword puzzle.

ACROSS

1. Both physical and _____ practice are important factors in badminton pre-game preparation.
2. Warm-up should increase _____ .
3. Physiologically warm-up increases the speed and force of _____ contraction.
4. General court _____ should be carefully analyzed during pre-game warm-up.
5. Warm-up is an _____ matter.

DOWN

1. _____ is an important aspect of badminton warm-up.
2. Look for the opponent's strengths and _____ during pre-game warm-up.
3. Both _____ and physiological warm-up prepare the badminton player.
4. _____ action is an important source of power in badminton and should be employed during warm-up.
5. _____ should not set in during warm-up time.

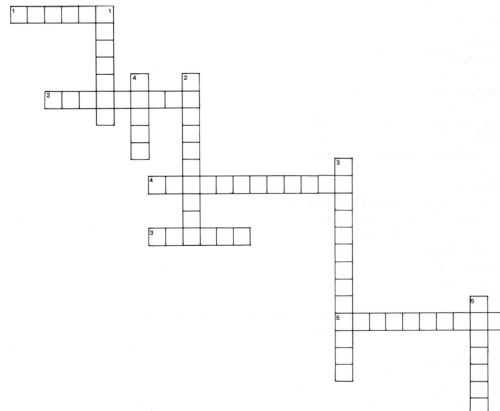

The Basic Fundamentals of Badminton

3

The Grip

The importance of the application of a proper gripping technique in badminton cannot be over-emphasized. The proper grip is necessary in order to ensure that enough force can be gathered through the range of motion of the "complete" badminton swing. Two critical components of the badminton swing which are affected greatly by application of an improper grip are the wrist snap and forearm rotation. Proper gripping technique enables the participant to employ the maximum wrist snap and forearm rotation which are needed to return most badminton placements and especially those to the deep backhand corner of the court.

Forehand

*The following explanations are for the right handed participant. If you are a left handed player, please reverse the following analyses. Hold the racket by its shaft with the left hand so that the racket strings are running up and down and the plane of the racket head is perpendicular to the floor (Figure 3.1–3.3). With the right hand, shake hands with the racket grip so that the little finger and heel of the palm of the hand are anchored on the heel of the racket grip. This will allow maximum wrist snap and forearm rotation. The V formed by the thumb and index finger should bisect the top wide bevel of the racket and be directly in line with the edge of the racket head (Figure 3.4 and 3.5). The racket should be firmly but not tightly gripped by the fingers rather than the palm of the hand. This will again insure maximum wrist and forearm action. The fingers should be slightly spread with the index finger secured in a trigger type position and the thumb comfortably wrapped around the grip. Do not place the index finger up behind the shaft of the racket as this will impede maximum wrist and forearm action. The racket should be held firmly upon impact with the shuttle unless employing a finesse shot. The grip should be comfortable and may be modified to meet individual comfort requirements. You may also obtain this forehand grip by holding the racket shaft in the nondominant hand with the racket head again perpendicular to the ground. Then place the dominant hand palm first on the racket face and slide the hand down the shaft and grip the handle as described previously.

[handwritten margin note, upper right:] wrist snap & forearm rotation

[handwritten note after "Forehand":] V bisects top wide bevel of racket & in line w/ edge of racket head

[handwritten note, bottom right:] index finger up behind shaft of racket impedes maximum wrist & forearm action

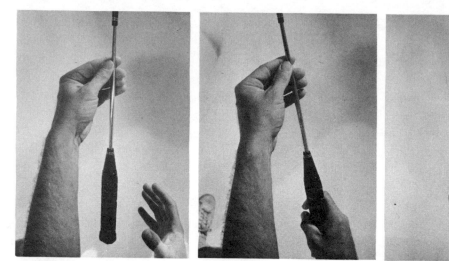

Figure 3.1 **Figure 3.2** **Figure 3.3**

Figures 3.1–3.3. Application of forehand grip.

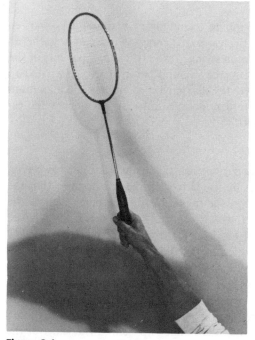

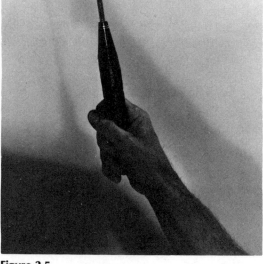

Figure 3.4 **Figure 3.5**

Figures 3.4 and 3.5. The forehand grip.

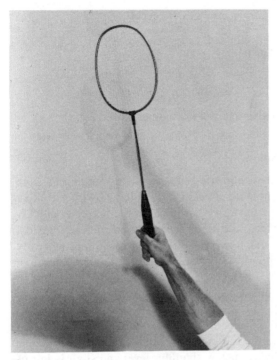

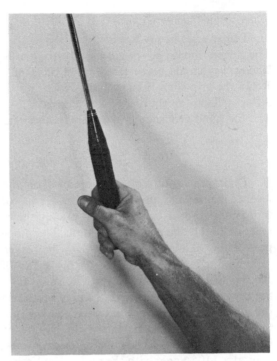

Figure 3.6

Figure 3.7

Figures 3.6 and 3.7. The backhand grip.

Backhand   *V moved to left (counterclockwise), bisects left top bevel of racket*

   Some players find that they can execute most badminton stroke variations without altering the forehand grip. Most players, however, do alter their grip for strokes to the left side of the body. (An exception may be the round-the-head overhead shot employed by the advanced player.) The backhand grip is executed by first assuming the proper forehand grip. The V formed by the thumb and index finger is then moved to the left or counterclockwise until the V bisects the left top bevel of the racket. With the exception of the thumb, the fingers should remain basically the same as in the forehand grip. The pad of the thumb should be positioned against the back bevel of the racket in order to impart more force when striking the shuttle (Figures 3.6 and 3.7). In actuality you are rotating the racket head about one-eighth of a turn to the right and re-gripping the handle. Some players also prefer to position the side of the thumb diagonally across the back bevel of the racket. Comfort, power and effectiveness should determine which backhand grip should be adopted.

Continental   *always somewhere between forehand & backhand grips*

   For some players a grip somewhere between the forehand and backhand or the continental grip is employed. It varies from player to player, but the continental grip is always somewhere between the forehand and backhand grips. The continental grip needs never to be changed and can be successfully employed in both forehand and backhand striking patterns. It is suggested that the player experiment to determine which gripping technique is most effective in relationship to power, accuracy and comfort.

Suggestions Concerning the Grip

Hold the racket firmly but not tightly.
The fingers should be spread slightly, trigger finger grip.
The racket should be an extension of the arm.
Relax the grip slightly to cock the wrist.
After striking the shuttle, relax the grip.
The forehand grip should approximate the Eastern grip utilized in tennis.

Ready Position

Due to the nature of the game of badminton, it is requisite that the player maintain a high level of mental and physical awareness. This constant state of readiness combined with the effort to maintain proper court position, usually the center court area, will enable the player to quickly respond to the demands of the game. The proper court posture or the ready position is a critical part of the "readiness factor" which the player should strive to achieve. In assuming the ready position, the player's feet, which form the base of support, should be positioned slightly wider than the shoulder width of the player. The knees are slightly flexed at approximately a 135° angle with the player's weight evenly distributed on the balls of the feet. The shoulder girdle is parallel to the net and there is slight flexion at the hip (waist). This position of readiness enables the player to maintain the proper balance and facilitates rapid movement in all directions. The arms should be extended from the body and carried approximately waist high. The elbow should be flexed or bent at a 110° angle with the racket head raised slightly below shoulder level and slightly left of the midline of the body (Figures 3.8 and 3.9). Eye contact should be exclusively focused on the shuttle. The ready position described and pictured will vary somewhat among individuals and alter appropriately in the game of doubles, but it is important that the above guidelines be kept in mind for all game situations.

Figure 3.9. The ready position.

Figure 3.8-3.9. The ready position.

Suggestions Concerning the Ready Position

✓Keep your eye on the shuttle.

✓Keep your racket head up.

Be relaxed.

✓Be on the balls of your feet with weight evenly distributed.

Wait until the opponent strikes the shuttle before moving, or move before it is struck if the opponent "telegraphs" the shot.

✓The ready position is usually associated with center court position which is astride the center line and 2–3 feet or 1 meter from the short service line.

The ready position will alter in the game of doubles and may become shot situation specific.

Footwork

goal to enable player to rapidly & efficiently move to proper court position to return shuttle

Footwork is a key factor in any sport and badminton is no exception. The goal of proper *effectively &* footwork is to enable the player to move rapidly and efficiently to the proper court position where *return to* the shuttle can be returned effectively and the player can return to center court position. Proper *center court position* technique concerning footwork begins with the player assuming the proper ready position in the center court area. The ready position is often described as a bouncing position on the balls of the feet while waiting to spring into action. From this vantage point there are seven basic footwork patterns which usually must be employed during a match (Figures 3.10–3.13). The footwork

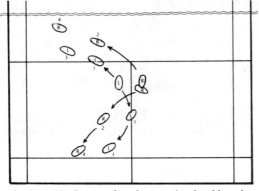

Figure 3.10. Forward and retreating backhand footwork patterns.

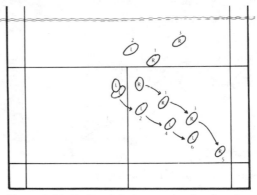

Figure 3.11. Forward and retreating forehand footwork patterns.

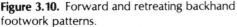
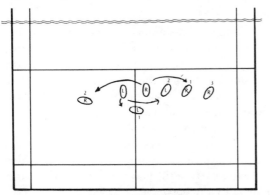

Figure 3.12. Lateral footwork pattern.

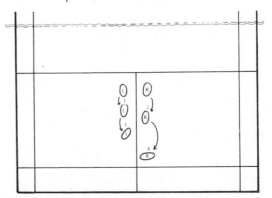

Figure 3.13. Backward footwork pattern.

Figure 3.14

Figure 3.15

Figure 3.16

Figure 3.17

Figure 3.18

Figure 3.19

Figures 3.14–3.19. Movement patterns.

movement patterns as diagrammed in Figures 3.10–3.13 and pictured in Figures 3.14–3.19 should be performed in rhythmic skipping, sliding, running or backpedaling motions depending on the amount of time that the player has to reach the shuttle and from what court position the shuttle is to be played. When playing most shots the player's hips and shoulders will be facing the appropriate side line after the first step is taken. The lead foot is usually the foot to the same side that the shuttle is to be played. When striking shots that require a large amount of force, the player should rotate the hips and shoulders from the side line toward the net. This rotary motion serves to generate more force for the shot return as well as to begin the player's movement back to proper center court position. Because of the speed of the game, it is recommended that the player use small shuffling steps when returning to the center court position. While returning to the proper court position, the player should at all times be facing the net with eyes focused on the shuttle. It is possible that the player will not be able to return to the desired center court position before the opponent returns the shuttle. When this situation arises, the player should stop, assume a low ready position and wait until the shuttle is played by the opponent.

16

Proper footwork will enable the player to reach an effective striking position as soon as possible, allowing the player to attack the shuttle in a higher position and therefore create more offensive options for the attacking player. For some individuals proper footwork technique is natural but for most players the fast and fluid footwork required by the game of badminton must be practiced until the proper footwork movement patterns become effective, efficient and effortless. It is helpful to practice footwork technique such as the side shuffle, cariocas, grass drills, backward step and flow as well as other agility drills in both warm-up and practice game situations. Wave drills and mirror drills also focus on footwork as does a high clear, overhead drop-hairpin, underhand net clear drill with continuous footwork pattern changing from one shot to the next. For more footwork ideas attend to the drills section in Chapters 4 through 11.

Suggestions Concerning Footwork

Always maintain a ready position and proper center court position.
Keep your eyes on the shuttle at all times.
Do not turn your back on the play.
Get to the shuttle as fast as possible.
Strive to get behind the shuttle before striking.
Transfer the weight from the back foot to the front foot when executing most shots.
Use shuffle steps when distance and time are not critical. Employ step outs, lead steps and cross over steps when you need to cover a greater distance in a short period of time.
Practice using various footwork drills will benefit both the technical skill (shot making) as well as tactical (strategy) dimension of your game. It's also physiologically beneficial.

Court Position

During a rally the ready position is usually assumed approximately two to three feet or one meter in back of the short service line. The feet are positioned on either side of the center line. This means that the player in the ready position and in the proper center court position will be approximately 9.5 feet or 2.90 meters from the net and 12.5 feet or 3.80 meters from the back boundary line (Figures 3.20–3.21). The reason for this court position is that it requires the shuttle coming off the opponent's racket less time to reach its destination to the short service area than it takes the shuttle to reach the back boundary area. The player, therefore, has less time to react and to move the shorter distance to retrieve a net shot and more time to retrieve the longer deep clear placements. The court position may be modified according to the strength of the player's or the opponent's game and style of play. During a service return, in singles, you position yourself at a slight angle with the heel of the left foot against the center line or sideline depending on where you are receiving serve since this cuts off the angle to your backhand.

Court position will vary while playing the game and on-court position adjustments are an intricate part of the game. An example of modified court position is the court position assumed by the attacking player after placing an effective drop shot close to the net and to the middle of the opponent's court. The attacking player may adjust his or her court position by moving a step closer to the net. This court adjustment is possible because the opponent can return only a drop shot or a high but shallow clear shot because of the difficulty of the placement of the shuttle in relationship to the net. See Figure 3.21 for the approximate court positions assumed after various shots have been placed and the Basic Situation and Striking Pattern Option and Position Chart on page 24 for further examples of fundamental play and position.

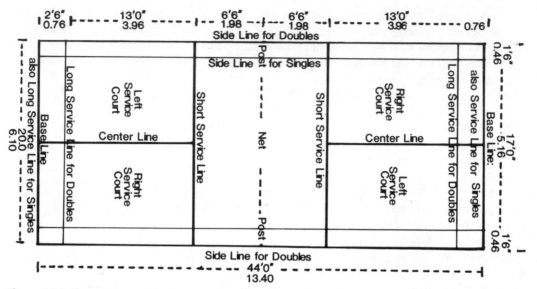

Figure 3.20. Court measurements.

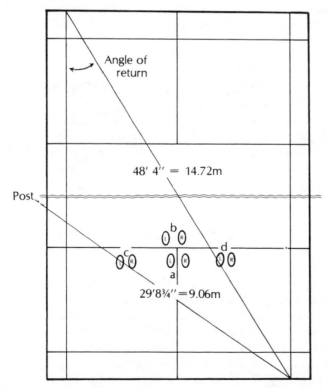

Figure 3.21. (a) Proper singles court position and ready position; (b) on-court position after drop shot; (c) on-court position after deep clear shot to opponent's forehand; (d) and on-court position after deep clear shot to opponent's backhand.

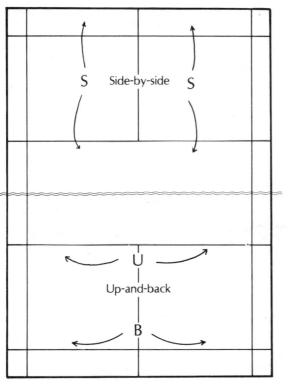

Figure 3.22. Double's court positions.

Doubles Court Coverage

There are two basic doubles formations that are used in doubles competition. These formations are the side-by-side (S) and the up-and-back (U-B) formations as shown in Figure 3.22. It is recommended for beginning players that the side-by-side formation be utilized. The side-by-side formation allows the court responsibilities to be divided in half by the center line and confusion over court position is kept to a minimum. Side-by-side works well when both players on a team are about equal in ability. The (S) court coverage style is also an important defensive alignment at all levels of play.

The up-and-back formation is more complex than the side-by-side formation. It is an attacking formation as compared to the side-by-side position which is a key to effective doubles play. The responsibilities of court coverage in the up-and-back formation (U-B) are pictured in Figure 3.22. The player's role may be divided evenly between the up-and-back partners, however, some doubles teams attempt to position the more skillful or powerful player in the B position. The up-and-back formation may also be a useful formation if one of the partners is less skilled or is an effective net or up player. No matter which formation is employed, on-court communication and adjustments will have to be made during play. As players become more experienced, a continuous switching and flowing combination of the two basic formations result. Thus doubles court coverage becomes almost personalized and unique formations appropriate to the game situations and doubles teams' strengths and weaknesses are developed.

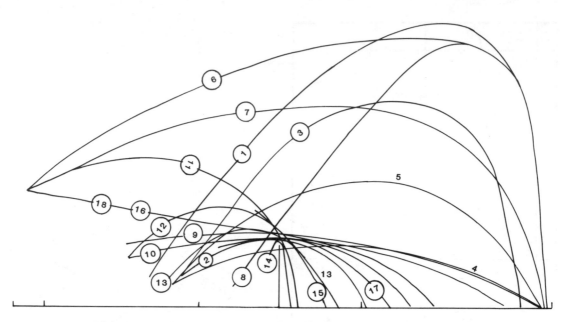

Figure 3.23. Flight patterns of the basic shots of badminton (1–18).

1. High deep singles serve
2. Low short doubles serve
3. High doubles serve
4. Drive serve
5. Flick serve
6. Defensive clear
7. Attacking clear
8. Underhand clear
9. Fast drive
10. Midcourt drive
11. Overhead drop
12. Underhand drop
13. Drive drop
14. Hairpin drop
15. Net smash
16. Half smash
17. Push shot
18. Smash

Suggestions Concerning Court Position

Know the court dimensions and utilize them to assume proper court position. (Figure 3.20).

Know the flight patterns of the various shots in badminton. (Figure 3.23).

Know the opponent's and partner's strengths and weaknesses.

Play your strengths and the opponent's weaknesses in order to maintain proper court position and advantage.

Know the opponent's and your basic striking pattern options to assume and maintain proper court position and balance.

Basic Striking Patterns of Badminton

In order to play the game of badminton effectively the player must build a repertoire of basic strokes. In badminton there are three basic striking patterns which the player should attempt to master in order to develop the basic shots. These striking patterns include the overhead, underhand and the drive or side arm. Development of these basic movement patterns will enable the player to serve, drive, clear, smash and drop as well as to incorporate any number of deceptive variations of these basic shots. Descriptions of the basic shots may be found in later sections. The desired flight patterns of the basic shots of badminton may be found below in Figure 3.23.

Figure 3.24. The forehand overhead.   **Figure 3.25.** The wrist snap.

Forehand Overhead

The basic forehand overhead striking pattern is used when executing shots such as the forehand clear, drop, drive and smash. The basic striking pattern of all forehand overhead strokes is the same with the only difference being in the angle of projection in respect to the shuttle and the face of the racket head and the force with which the shuttle is struck at the point of contact. When the shuttle is placed by an opponent to the player's forehand side, the player must move from the ready position to the court position where the shuttle is placed. The proper footwork techniques have been described earlier in this chapter. The proper footwork will enable the player to assume a position behind the flight of the shuttle. In this position the player's feet are almost parallel to the net and point to the forehand side line. The left shoulder will be pointing toward the net. As the player moves to attain this position the racket arm is drawn behind the head and shoulders as if to scratch the back with the racket head. The forehand grip is employed and the wrist is cocked causing the racket head to point downward while the right hand and grip of the racket will be maintained near the right ear. This backswing action will simultaneously rotate the shoulder and the hips from left to right. As this occurs the body weight is placed on the rear or right foot. The backswing process may vary in speed, time and position, depending on the amount of time the player has to reach and strike the shuttle.

In order to strike the shuttle, the body weight will be transferred from the rear to the front foot as the front foot steps forward toward the net and the arm is extended to reach the shuttle at its highest point. This action will cause rotation of the shoulders and hips from right to the left side (Figure 3.24). This rotation will bring the player's chest to a position facing the net. The shuttle is thus contacted in front of this position and with a fully extended arm. As contact is initiated the wrist will uncock and the forearm will rotate medially or to the inside and the shuttle will be projected by the face of the racket head depending on which of the basic shots is to be employed. The proper follow through also depends on the type of shot selected. It is important that all forehand striking patterns look identical in order to deceive and to keep the opponent off balance especially when a finesse shot is to be employed. The wrist snap is a combination of medial rotation and flexion of the wrist along with medial rotation of the forearm. It is important not to just flex the wrist—with a combination of rotation and flexion a greater range of motion is achieved and thus more power and force is produced (Figure 3.25).

21

Backhand Overhead

The basic backhand overhead striking pattern is used when executing shots such as the backhand clear (primarily), drop, drive and smash. Unlike the forehand overhead, the backhand overhead striking pattern seems to be less powerful for most players and may cause some difficulty. It is, therefore, extremely important to be in proper court position when striking the shuttle. The backhand overhead pattern is the same for all backhand overhead shots with again the only discernible difference being the point of contact in relation to the shuttle and the face of the racket head as well as the amount of force with which the shuttle is struck.

When the shuttle is placed by the opponent to the player's backhand side, the player moves from the ready position to the court position where the shuttle is placed. The proper footwork technique has again been discussed previously.

The proper footwork will enable the player to assume a position behind the flight of the shuttle. In this position the player's feet will be almost parallel to the net and point to the backhand side line. The player's right shoulder will be pointing toward the net. As the player moves to attain this position, the racket head is moved from that of the ready position and is dropped as the right elbow is flexed or bent and pointed in the direction of the on-coming shuttle. The racket arm is also drawn back with the right hand until the racket grip approximates the left shoulder. The backhand grip is employed which will restrict the wrist cocking action which is why the elbow position is so important. This backswing action will cause a right to left rotation in the shoulder and hip region. As this rotation occurs, the body weight is placed on the rear or left foot. The backswing process may vary in speed, time and position, depending on the amount of time the player has to reach and strike the shuttle.

In order to strike the shuttle the body weight is shifted forward as a step is taken toward the net with the right foot. The shoulders and hips rotate from left to right as the racket arm starts to extend forward. The shuttle is contacted well in front of the body plane with an extended arm. The elbow leads this striking pattern and as contact is made at a fully extended arm position the wrist is snapped and the forearm laterally rotated or rotated to the outside as the wrist turns over. The face of the racket head meets the shuttle at the highest extension point and the shuttle is projected according to the type of shot that is to be employed. This is exceedingly important since the higher the contact with the shuttle the less force is needed to propel the shuttle since it will travel a shorter distance than if you would allow it to drop to a lower position. The follow through also depends on the type of shot selected. The timing of the shift of weight, shoulder and hip rotation, arm extension, wrist snap and the forearm rotation is vital in order to generate enough force to return the shuttle from a deep court position. It should also be noted that many times, especially when employing an overhead clear shot, the shot is executed with the shuttle above or even behind the player allowing no time for backswing or body rotation. Of course, this requires advanced skill level and tremendous forearm and wrist capability. The development of a powerful striking pattern takes time and practice but in order to be an effective player a sound and efficient backhand is perhaps the most vital component.

Underhand

The underhand striking pattern is used when the shuttle must be contacted below the level of the net and an upward striking motion is necessary in order to project the shuttle over the net. The underhand striking pattern is employed as a defensive measure and usually takes place after the opponent has hit an effective smash or drop shot. The primary shots requiring the underhand striking pattern include the serve, clear and the drop. The same basic fundamentals as described

Figure 3.26. The underhand clear shot.

in the forehand and backhand overhead striking patterns in relation to the footwork, hip and shoulder, arm, wrist and forearm movement may be applied to the forehand and backhand underhand striking pattern. It should be noted that most underhand shots do not require a backswing (excluding the high deep serve and clear) and are primarily blocking or flicking type shots. For this reason most shots necessitating the underhand striking pattern are placed between the opponent's short service line and the net. This, of course, requires a great deal of precision allowing very little margin for error.

If there is ample time for the player to take a backswing, the racket is drawn back to a position in back of the player. The tip of the racket head is placed in a back scratching position and lies between the player's scapulae or shoulder blades. The racket head is maintained approximately at the shoulder level with the right hand or grip held slightly higher than the racket head. The right hand or racket grip will be positioned near the right or left shoulder, depending on whether forehand or backhand, and the thumb will point toward the back boundary line. The racket arm is flexed or bent with the elbow pointing toward the ground on the forehand side or toward the on-coming shuttle if the shuttle is to the player's backhand side. The wrist is cocked and ready for action. As the weight shifts forward, the racket head is brought downward and forward until the arm is fully extended as the forearm and wrist action take place and the shuttle is contacted. At this point of contact the racket face will be almost parallel to the ground. Although the shuttle is contacted below the level of the net, it is vital that the player strike the shuttle at its highest possible position. The follow through is imparted in the direction of the flight of the shuttle and will terminate in the area of the left or right shoulder. Remember, it is not totally an underhand pendulum swing—it approaches a combination sidearm/underarm striking pattern. This non-pendulum swing is important in order to obtain maximum force in hitting the shuttle (Figure 3.26).

Drive or Side Arm

The drive is an attacking stroke primarily employed when the shuttle is between shoulder and waist in height and the shuttle position makes it impossible or impractical for an effective overhead or underhand striking pattern to be employed. The striking pattern of the drive is similar to that of the side arm baseball throw. The same basic fundamentals as discussed with the forehand and backhand overhead and the underhand striking patterns in regard to the footwork, hip and shoulder, arm, wrist and forearm movement may be applied to the forehand and backhand drive or side arm.

23

Basic Situation and Striking Pattern Option and Position Chart

Situation	Shuttle Position	Striking Pattern	Placement of On-Court Return	Rationale	Opponent Shot Options	On-Court Recovery Position
Back Court	High	Smash	straight, center or cross court	to hit winner	Block	center court
		Half Smash	straight or center	deceive opponent	Clear	shallow center court
		Drop Shot	straight or cross court	force a pop-up or lift	Clear	shallow center court
		Attacking Clear	deep corners or center	to surprise opponent	Smash, clear or drop	midcourt
	Low	Defensive Clear	deep center	provide recovery time	Smash, clear, or drop	center court
Midcourt	High	Smash	opponents backhand side	to hit winner	Block	shallow center court
	Shoulder Height	Drive or push shot	straight, center or cross court	decrease opponents recovery time	Block	shallow center court
	Low	Defensive clear or block	deep center	force opponent to back court and gain recovery time	smash, clear, drop	midcourt
		Drop Shot	cross court or center	force pop-up	drop, pop-up, or clear	deep front court
Front Court	High/Shoulder Height	Net smash, dump or push (brush or dab) shot	opponents backhand side	to hit winner	pop-up or weak block	deep front court
	Below net	Drop, hairpin, or variations	straight or cross court and close to net	to force pop-up or weak clear	drop or clear	shallow center court
	Low	Defensive clear	center	to force opponent deep and gain recovery time	smash, clear, or drop	center court

Adapted from Downey, J. "An Analysis of the Game" *Badminton USA*, November, 1979.

Figure 3.27. Foot patterns.

The movement of the backswing is essentially the same as that of the underhand striking pattern. When the racket head is drawn backward from the ready position, the racket arm is flexed or bent at the elbow. The right hand or racket grip is drawn to a position near the right shoulder for a forehand drive and the left shoulder to employ a backhand drive. The pattern of the forward swing is led by the elbow action and the full arm extension, forearm and wrist movements are similar to the forehand and backhand overhead arm movement. The point of contact with the shuttle is to the side and in front of the body and the racket face will be parallel to the net as contact is made. The follow through is in the direction of the shuttle and the player will find that the racket grip will move across the body at about shoulder level ending in the area of the left or right shoulder. If the shuttle is contacted properly, the shuttle will skim the net and remain parallel to the floor forcing the opponent to employ a weak return.

With all striking patterns of the game of badminton it is requisite that the player summate all forces in order to gain maximal efficiency and effectiveness. This requires a number of factors including agility, speed, timing, coordination, dedication to practice and knowledge of the game. The following chart of the basic situations and striking pattern options available to the player is meant to facilitate your badminton progress. The chart is by no means complete in nature but provides you with some fundamentals to make the game more exciting and enjoyable.

Suggestions for Basic Striking Patterns

All shots should look identical until the last possible second when the shuttle contacts the racket face.

Employ all sources of power including body weight transfer, hip, shoulder and trunk rotation, back swing, follow through and wrist action for maximal efficiency and effectiveness.

Practice each basic striking pattern 25 times per side and improvement will be noticeable.

Creative Tips

Paint grips on racket handles with latex paint. Paint hand with latex paint and then grip racket properly and tightly for 10 seconds, release grip and allow to dry. Different grips can be placed on same racket handle using different color latex paint (i.e., backhand, continental, etc.). This gives students a pattern to follow and helps to maintain proper grip.

Place basic footwork patterns on court using athletic or plastic tape. Actually outline footprints with tape and employ arrows so that students can practice basic footwork patterns with a template to follow. (Figure 3.27.)

Court positioning can be aided by using squares on targets with helpful hints written in them. This may be permanently painted on floor and then sealed.

Paint various striking patterns and shuttlecock trajectories on walls so the student has visual aids in shuttlecock striking and flight patterns.

Cartoons are also helpful if painted in appropriate spots with helpful hints such as "Keep your eye on the shuttle."

Tape areas on the court to project the various basic serves and striking patterns. Keep a progress chart and set goals.

Thought Provoker

Match the items in column I with an item in column II. Provide your reasoning for the selection (why?).

Column I

A. A grip between the forehand and backhand grip. Why? (Reasoning)

B. The shoulders are _____ to the net when in the ready position. Why?

C. _____ court position is important to maintain throughout a match. Why?

D. The fingers should be _____ in any badminton grip. Why?

E. When beginning players are of equal ability _____ strategy should be employed. Why?

F. Wrist snap may best be described as _____ . Why?

G. _____ is the major factor in power of advanced players. Why?

H. The action of the underhand clear shot can be likened to a _____ . Why?

I. All shots look identical until the racket _____ _____ . Why?

Column II

Arm action
Western
Vertical
Back court
Up-and-back
Center court
Flexion
Hits shuttle
Spread
Together
Continental
Underhand, pendulum swing
Wrist snap
Parallel
Rotation-flexion
Side-by-side
Starts forward
Combination side-underhand swing

The Serve

4

The serve is an underhand stroke that is used to place the shuttle into play. It is also the only shot in badminton where a player has full control over the shuttle before attempting to strike it. The serve may be placed into play by either a forehand or backhand stroke. Because the shuttle must be projected upwards in order to clear the net, unlike other racket sports, the serve is classified as a defensive shot.

In regard to the service, Law 14a states, "If in serving, the shuttle at the instant of being struck be higher than the server's waist, or if at the instant of being struck the shaft of the racket be not pointing in a downward direction to such an extent that the whole of the head of the racket is discernibly below the whole of the server's hand holding the racket," then the serve is not legal. Figure 4.1 shows the proper hand and racket position necessary for a legal service. For a serve to be legal, the server's feet must be touching the ground and in a stationary position until the serve is delivered. The server must also be in the proper service court and may not be in contact with any of the service court lines.

The server's position (Figure 4.2) may vary, but in singles competition the server usually assumes a position approximately three feet or one meter behind the short service line and just to the right or left of the center line with the feet almost touching the line. The positional depth of the server is dictated to some degree by the server's power and the resulting flight pattern of the shuttlecock. If most high deep serves go long and out of the court, one can step back slightly and if the shuttle is falling very short inside the baseline, the server should move forward a step or two. In doubles the server's position is about a foot and a half or one half meter closer to the short service line than the singles position as the server is responsible for covering the net shot returns while the server's partner will cover the back court area. If employing side-by-side tactics, the doubles server will move back some in the court.

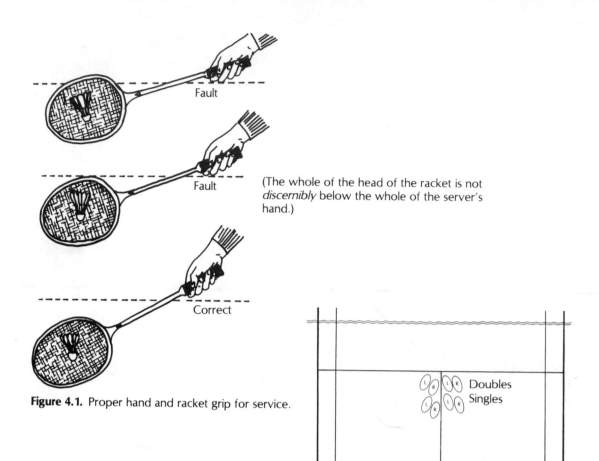

Fault

Fault

(The whole of the head of the racket is not *discernibly* below the whole of the server's hand.)

Correct

Figure 4.1. Proper hand and racket grip for service.

Doubles
Singles

Figure 4.2. Server's positions for singles and doubles.

The Starting Position

The server stands in an erect position with the feet spread shoulder width apart and the left foot placed in front of the right. The left foot should be pointing to the center of the receiver's court and the right foot maintained at a 45°–90° angle with the center line. The weight is placed on the rear or right foot. The shuttle is held in the left hand between the thumb and index finger which are positioned lightly on the shuttle where the cork and the feathers join. The nose of the shuttle is pointed directly toward the playing surface so that when the shuttle is released it will fall straight down. The server's left arm is extended in front of the body about waist height with the left shoulder pointing toward the center of the receiver's court. The right shoulder will be pointing backwards. The racket is held with the forehand or continental grip, wrist cocked and positioned with the grip about waist high and the racket head slightly below waist height and in back of the right foot.

Figure 4.3

Figure 4.4

Figure 4.5

Figure 4.6

Figure 4.7

Figures 4.3–4.7. Server's striking pattern.

Service Striking Sequence

As the shuttle is released from the left hand, the server's weight is transferred from the rear or right foot to the front or left foot and the racket is brought back so the tip of the racket head will be pointing toward the back boundary line. Simultaneously, the shoulders and hips will rotate from right to left as the racket is swung in a sweeping motion downward and forward. At the point of contact with the shuttle, which should occur legally as close to waist height as possible, the server's shoulders will be facing the receiver's court, the wrist will uncock and the forearm will medially rotate or pronate toward the midline of the body. The follow through should be imparted in the desired direction of the flight of the shuttle and will usually end over the server's left shoulder. The service striking pattern should resemble an underhand pendulum action which is slightly modified to the side. This striking pattern will yield increased power for high deep serves and can also be used for lower shuttle trajectory across the net for low short serves. (Figures 4.3–4.7)

Strategy

When serving in singles, the serve most commonly employed is the high deep serve to the backhand side of the receiver's service court. The backhand is usually a trouble spot for the opponent. In doubles because of the shortened length of the receiver's service court the most frequently used serve is the low short serve to the intersection of the center line and short service line of the opponent or a serve to the intersection of the outside sideline and short service line of the opponent. This shuttle placement gives the opponent less of an angle of return which increases the probability that the server or the server's partner will be able to effectively play the service return. Two other types of serves which are often employed if the opponent is crowding the net are the drive serve and the combination serve. Each is placed to the receiver's backhand side with the drive serve being propelled as fast and close to the net as possible while the combination serve is placed above the reach of the outstretched racket arm of the opponent. The drive and combination serves are dangerous and should be employed sparingly and only in the appropriate situations (when the opponent crowds the net) by experienced players. Another serve which is a recent development is the flick serve. This serve takes two forms, basically it is a low short serve, but can also be hit similar to a combination serve if the opponent crowds the front of the service court. The basic flick serve is employed by experienced doubles players. The server stands next to the short service line in the center line corner with shoulders parallel to the net, feet shoulder width apart, and toes pointing toward net. The racket is held with the proper grip and turned so that the head is down with the backhand facing the opponent. The handle is held about chest high. The head of the racket is held below the waist. (Figure 4.8) The movement action is a slight extension and lateral rotation of the wrist—a flick. This keeps the shuttle very close to the top of the net and very near the short service line of your opponent. The net camouflages the shuttle and the shuttle travels the shortest possible legal distance from your short service line to your opponent's just barely clearing the net. This gives the opponent the least amount of time to react to the serve. The server is also in an advantageous position to step up to play net. This is a relatively easy serve to master because of the amount of movement involved. It does take a little time to get the right touch. Too little flick results in a net serve and too much flick often results in a returned smash. If the opponent crowds the short service line, a more forceful flick resulting in combination serve may be effectively employed.

Suggestions Concerning the Serving Strategy

It is important that the proper flight pattern be realized when serving. (Figure 3.23)

The high deep serve should be hit high and fall straight downward as close as possible to the long service line.

The short low serve should be guided just over the net so the shuttle is on its downward flight as it passes the net.

The low serve is used most frequently (approximately 90%) in doubles.

The deep serve is primarily employed in singles play.

The flick serve is used when the opponent is crowding the net but is difficult to master.

For the drive serve to be legal you should stand deeper in the court.

Know your court dimensions.

Figure 4.8. The flick serve.

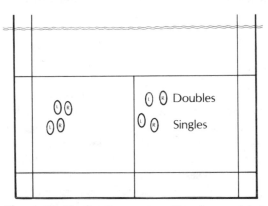

Doubles

Singles

Figure 4.9. The proper court position for receiving the serve in singles and doubles.

Receiving the Serve

Receiving the serve is a very critical part of the game. Because the serve is not an offensive shot, the object is to prevent the receiver from making an offensive return. The receiving position for singles should be approximately six feet or two meters from the short service line and just off the center line. If the serve is to the left service court, the receiver's position should be approximately one to two feet or .046 meters from the singles sideline and six feet or two meters in back of the short service line (Figure 4.9). This position will enable the receiver to return most of the serves with the forehand and also enable the receiver to deal with the high deep serve usually employed in singles competition. A straight clear or overhead drop is typically the best return of an effective high deep service. The ready position described in Figures 3.8 and 3.9 or some of the many specialized variations should be employed while waiting for the serve.

In doubles the receiver's position is usually approximately one to three feet or one meter in back of the short service line with the racket head up and in the ready position. Most doubles serves are the low short variety and should be met as soon as possible by the receiver. The low short serves are usually returned with a drop shot or push shot down the closest side line.

Service to the Proper Court and Scoring

In singles competition serving and receiving the serve is a relatively simple procedure. If the server's score is 0 or an even number, the service is directed from the right service court to the opponent's right service court. If the server's score is an odd number, the service is directed from the left service court to the opponent's left service court. If the server wins the point, the server switches to the other service court and continues back and forth until the service is lost or a "Service Over" occurs.

The scoring for doubles is slightly more complex. The team that serves first must always serve from the right service court into the opponent's right service court. The team that serves first has only one term of service. Thereafter, each team member will receive an opportunity to serve in each inning until the end of the game. In doubles your team's score dictates which team member should serve or receive the serve and in which service court each player is to be positioned. The first service of each inning must begin from the right service court into the opponent's right service court. If your team's score is 0 or an even number then you and your partner should be in the respective service courts in which you started the game and serve and receive the first service accordingly. The partner who began the game in the right service court will serve first (first server) from the right service court position, if the score is 0 or even. If the team's score is odd then the partner whose original position was in the left service court will move to the right hand service court and serve first. After a point is scored, the service courts are alternated just as in a singles game. When the first server loses the serve, the second player will serve from the court he/she is in without rotation. The second server will continue the service and the service procedure until the second server loses the serve and the serve is given to the opponents. The serving and receiving procedure is then repeated. The paramount rule in doubles service rotation is that you only switch sides when your team scores a point and you can only score points when your team is serving. The receiving team never rotates and if the serving team did not win a point the second server serves without rotation.

The player's team that wins the game always serves first in the next game. After each game in a doubles match, the teams may or may not alter their service and receiving sequence, but these positions must remain intact for the entire game. For further information concerning the serving and scoring in the game of badminton the reader should consult the section of this text concerning the Laws of Badminton.

Suggestions Concerning the Serve

The player can only score a point when serving, therefore the serve is important.
When serving watch the shuttle as contact is made with the racket face.
Be sure the head of the racket is below the hand and waist.
Concentration and confidence are important when serving.
When receiving the serve, concentration, aggression and anticipation are the important factors.
When receiving or serving, your team's score will dictate your court position.
When the score is even the individual who started service is in the right hand court.

Practice Techniques

1. Serve to partner who allows the shuttle to fall to the ground informing you of effectiveness and accuracy.
2. Serve to partner who attempts to offensively return the shuttle.
3. Serve to partner who mispositions himself/herself in order for the server to select the most advantageous serve.
4. Move your position and attempt different serves from different spots in your service areas.

Figure 4.10. Sample of mini-court model.

Common Errors

High Deep Serve

Hitting too short—lack of power.
Hitting too low and deep—racket face angle.

Low Short Serve

Hitting too high—racket face angle.
Hitting too deep—too much racket.
Hitting into net—racket face closed.

Creative Tips

Place numbers or targets on serving areas. Hit serves and allow them to land on targets or the numbers. The most effective serves receive highest point values.

Place strings above the net (tied to both net posts) running in the same plane as the net. One string 3″ above net and the others at varying intervals up to 4′ above the net (use extensions on poles if needed). This will enable you to practice trajectories of various serves in relation to the height of the net.

Use mini-courts (Figure 4.10) to assist in the understanding of scoring, positioning and service rotation.

Thought Provoker

Read the following fairy tale and extract any items that could be related to the badminton service.

Little Mary stood perfectly still and quiet with her back to the woods and with her feet comfortably apart. As the bear approached she bent over and picked up a stick and gripped it at one end while keeping the pointed end facing downward well below her waist. In a matter of seconds the huge bear was upon her and then they were side by side and Mary immediately slid forward so that they were now up and back from each other. Mary slowly slipped away by slightly bending her knees and waist as she quietly walked under the limbs always staying on the balls of her feet. She finally reached out with a sidearm-underarm action and grabbed a long hanging vine and climbed quickly up and out of the reach of the bear. She began to swing and after a number of back and forth swings she let go and went upward high and deep into the woods. Mary was never seen again but everytime one walks through the woods and flicks away the mosquitoes one remembers little Mary's flight and battle with the bear.

The Clear

5

The Defensive and Attacking Clears

The clear is the most frequently used power shot in the game of singles badminton and can be offensive or defensive in nature. The clear is hit from either the forehand or backhand side and powerfully propelled by any of the three basic striking patterns discussed in the previous chapter (the overhead, underhand, drive or side arm). The clear is basically a high deep shot to the opponent's baseline. At the point of contact with the shuttle, the racket face is forcefully exploded in an upward and forward direction. The shuttle will leave the racket face at a 90° angle. The shuttle is contacted a little later than in the execution of the drop or smash shot. An effective defensive clear shot will adopt a high and deep trajectory and fall straight down or perpendicular to the floor landing within 6 inches or one-sixth of a meter of the back boundary line (Figure 3.23). The primary objective of the defensive or high clear is to move the opponent deep into the backcourt and if possible to force the opponent to employ a weak return. Driving the opponent deep into the backcourt also enables the player to set up an effective drop shot as a follow-up shot selection. The drop shot will be discussed in a later section and is one way of drawing the opponent close to the net. As a defensive shot, because of the shuttle's high and deep flight patterns, the high clear enables the player ample time to regain the center court position and control the tempo or flow of the game.

If the opponent's position is close to the net, the attacking player often employs an attacking clear shot. The attacking clear is an offensive shot that travels in a somewhat lower trajectory than that of the normal high deep clear. In the attacking clear, the shuttle is placed just over the opponent's outstretched reach after which the shuttle will fall toward the back three feet or one meter of the court (Figure 3.23). The attacking clear will apply pressure on the opponent and if struck properly usually results in a point or a service change for the attacker. (Figures 5.1–5.6)

Figure 5.1.

Figure 5.2

Figure 5.3

Figure 5.4

Figure 5.5

Figure 5.6

Figures 5.1–5.6. The clear shot.

Suggestions Concerning the Clear

When striking a forehand clear shot, point the left arm in the direction of the oncoming shuttle. Strike the shuttle while pushing off on the rear or right foot.

Throw the racket head at the shuttle using all the force necessary for an effective placement. Have a natural and full follow through.

Be sure to use the proper trajectory depending on which type of clear shot is being employed. Hit the shuttle with maximum force.

Practice Techniques

Stand one-half to three-fourths back in the court and drop or toss the shuttle up and hit high clears. Partner on opposite side allows shuttles to hit floor and provides you with knowledge of results concerning their placement.

Same drill but this time partner starts shuttlecock and you hit it back with a high clear then the partner lets it drop to floor. Hit a number (10–15) of shots in succession on each drill.

Rally the shuttle back and forth employing alternate overhand, and underhand clearing striking patterns.

Repeat the above sequence concentrating on one clearing striking pattern.

Rally shuttlecock back and forth away from partner in order to make him/her move to shuttlecock before striking it.

Common Errors

Improper body position.
> Not turned sideways
> Pushing instead of hitting shuttlecock

Lack of wrist snap.

Not using all sources of power—not stepping—little or no backswing and trunk rotation.

Improper racket face angle.

Not watching the shuttle. (CONCENTRATE!)

Arm too rigid and straight (relax).

Little or no follow through.

Too much underhand pendulum pattern—modify striking pattern to side position.

Shuttlecock flight common errors

Too low trajectory and deep—racket face too closed (overhand) too open (underhand).

Too high and short—racket face too open (overhand) or in front of you (underhand).

Playing shuttle too far behind you (overhand) or in front of you (underhand).

Lack of power—wrist, step, follow through, windup, body position and rotation.

Creative Tips

Place marks of different colors or numbers on the floor and hit all types of clears toward your target. Have your partner let the clears drop and inform you of the colors or numbers that the shuttle lands on (Figure 5.7).

Grunt—On every defensive high clear grunt out loud so everyone can hear you. This helps awareness and provides for maximum effort thus maximum force on the shot.

Reach up high—Place lines on the wall next to the court (tape, string, paint, etc.). This will serve as a reminder for you to reach up above that line in order to hit an effective overhand high clear. Place a rectangle or trough on baseline—one foot wide all the way across the baseline (6″ inside, 6″ outside the baseline). Try to hit shuttles into the trough using effective clears (Figure 5.8).

Have your partner take a stop watch and time the "hang" time on your defensive or high clear shot.

Figure 5.7. Sample numbered targets.

Figure 5.8. Sample shuttle placement trough.

Thought Provoker

Take each of the following clear trajectory shot patterns and explain what is good and bad about each. How may each clearing striking pattern be altered to become more effective and like an ideal clear?

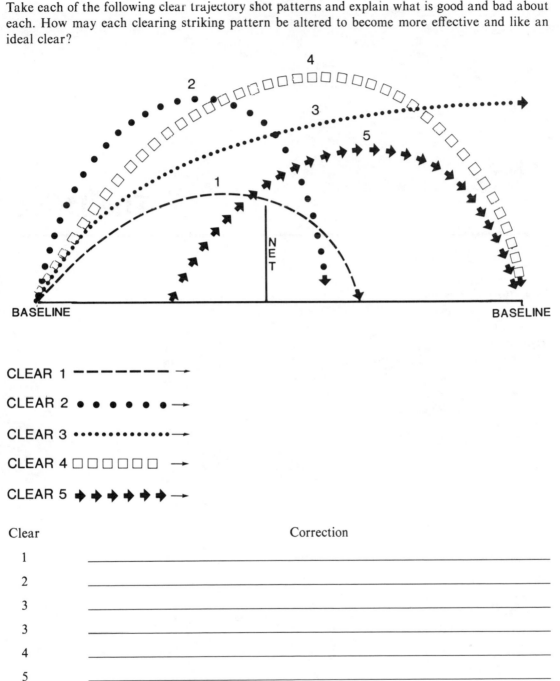

CLEAR 1 – – – – – – →

CLEAR 2 • • • • • →

CLEAR 3 ••••••••••→

CLEAR 4 ☐ ☐ ☐ ☐ ☐ ☐ →

CLEAR 5 ➔ ➔ ➔ ➔ ➔ →

Clear	Correction
1	
2	
3	
3	
4	
5	

The Drive

6

There are two basic drive shots which are commonly displayed in the game of badminton. The side arm and overhead drives. These drive shots incorporate either a powerful side arm or overhead striking pattern which may be applied from either the forehand or backhand side of the court. (Figures 6.1–6.6) The basic fundamentals of the drive shot have been described in Chapter 3. The shot travels parallel to the floor, close to the top of the net and always lands deep in relation to the opponent's baseline. The drive shot is used in both singles and doubles competition when the opponent is out of proper court position. The attacking player, in order to take instantaneous advantage of the opponent's poor court position, usually places the shuttle straight ahead, down the closest side line or cross court. If the attacking player elects to employ a cross court drive, it should be placed deep in the opponent's court and preferably to the opponent's backhand. The cross court drive, however, requires more time to reach its destination and may be intercepted by the opponent returning to proper center court position. The object of the drive is to force the opponent to make a weak return or to win a point outright.

There is also an underhand drive but this is not nearly as effective an offensive weapon as the sidearm or overhead drives since the shuttle must travel up to clear the net. This gives the shot less offensive punch and also allows the opponent more time to reach the shuttle for a return. The flight patterns of the sidearm, overhead and underhand drives may be found in Figure 3.15.

Figure 6.1

Figure 6.2

Figure 6.3

Figure 6.4

Figure 6.5

Figure 6.6

Figures 6.1–6.6. The backhand overhead drive shot.

Suggestions Concerning the Drive

Strike the shuttle at its highest possible trajectory.

Hit the shuttle down the closest side line or cross court.

The racket head should follow the flight of the shuttle.

The drive stance resembles a baseball batting stance.

The palm of the left hand is pointing to the ceiling on the forehand and to the floor in the backhand position just before the forward swing is initiated.

On contact with the shuttle the racket face or the strings of the racket will be parallel to the net.

Power is exceedingly important. Remember the drive is an offensive shot.

Practice Techniques

Your partner sets up high clear shots to the rear 1/4 of your back court. You return employing
the appropriate drive shot. Partner lets your return drop and gives you knowledge of results.

One person clears, one person drives alternately in a rally.

Drive at each other. Both partners stand about 3/4 of the way back in their respective courts.
Drive to both the forehand and backhand sides.

Common Errors

Hitting the shuttle too softly.

Not properly angling the racket face.

Not enough of a parallel trajectory on the shuttle.

No follow through.

Hitting out of court on the side arm and overhead drive.

Shuttlecock flight common errors.

Too deep—racket face too open or too closed depending on overhead or underhand drive.

Too short—racket face too closed.

Lack of power—wrist snap lacking.

Creative Tips

Rally drives against a wall aiming at a 6' high line. Keep the shuttle near the line and continue
to rally. Place a target standing about 1' high, 2' from baseline and attempt to hit the target
with drives.

Place a string across the net plane about 2' above the net. Rally keeping the shuttle between the
string and the net.

Add newspaper to the string so the area from the string to the net top is blocked. All effective
drives should hit the paper and fall to opponents side of court.

Throw styrofoam balls—sidearm, underhand and overhand to improve the basic drive striking
patterns.

Thought Provoker

Follow the maze so that you hit an effective drive at the completion of the maze. Answer the numbered fill-ins as you approach them respectively in the maze.

1. The most effective drive is the _____ .

2. The shuttle should land near the opponent's _____ to be an effective drive.

3. The trajectory of the shuttle should be _____ to the court for an effective drive.

4. The drive is an _____ shot.

5. The shuttle should stay _____ to the net in an effective drive.

6. Drives are hit both _____ and _____ the _____ .

The Drop

7

The drop shot is appropriately named as it is a relatively slow shot that just drops over the plane of the net and into the opponent's front court. Ideally the drop shot always lands in front of the opponent's short service line. The drop shot may be stroked from either the forehand or the backhand side of the court and may be struck with any of the three basic striking patterns (the overhand, underhand, drive or side arm) described in Chapter 3. The drop shot is very important in both singles and doubles competition as it is the only placement that will draw the opponent from center court position into the front court. The clear, drop and smash shots each employ the same basic mechanics in regard to the striking pattern so deception is a key ingredient in order to strike an effective drop. The drop shot should be softly guided over the net as compared to the powerfully propelled clear or smashing shot. In singles competition, strategy often dictates that an up and back game of court movement take place between the two opposing players. It is critical that the player is able to strike a strong and effective clearing or drive shot and also, using the same striking pattern, hit a deceptive drop shot. This is accomplished by applying a softer touch upon contact with the shuttle and guiding the shuttle gently over the net. The shot still takes an immediate downward trajectory and the power is lessened by not snapping the wrist. (Figures 7.1 and 7.2 for proper and improper racket head angles.)

Just as important as the deceptive overhead, underhand or side arm drop shot is the underhand net drop shot. The net drop shots are softly guided just over the net and usually angled to one corner of the opponent's front court. A straight ahead underhand net drop shot is called a hairpin because the trajectory that the shuttle assumes takes the form of a hairpin (Figure 3.23). The hairpin can be either offensive or defensive and is usually employed off of a drop shot or hairpin. To be effective, the underhand net drop shot must just clear the top of the net and immediately fall straight toward the floor; ideally the shuttle should crawl up the net, crawl over the top, and crawl down the opposite side of the net. The shuttle does most of the work to clear the net with very little wrist action employed. The shuttle is best contacted with the forehand racket face on the forehand side and the backhand face on the backhand side. Contact should be about waist high. The object of the underhand net drop shot like all drop shots is to force the opponent to

51

Figure 7.1. Proper racket face angle for the overhead drop shot.

Figure 7.2. Improper racket face angle for the overhead drop shot.

Figure 7.3. Underhand cross court drop shot from a deep position.

employ an underhand striking pattern (to hit up) with as little striking angle as possible. This enables the attacking player to move a step or two closer to the net from center court position in order to wait in anticipation for a weak underhand return (Figure 3.21). The closer the shuttle falls to the opponent's side of the net, the more difficult it is for the opponent to apply an effective deep underhand return. The one drawback that the drop shot has is that its pace is slow. This allows the opposing player more time to react and play the shuttle. It is recommended that when employing an effective drop shot that the opponent be deeper than proper center court position and that the shuttle be placed as far from the center of the court and the opponent as possible. Cross court underhand drop shots are employed with both the forehand and the backhand. The shot is performed best by keeping low to the ground and employing a snap of the wrist. The result should produce a flattened out trajectory (Figure 7.3).

Suggestions Concerning the Drop Shot

Be deceptive. Employ the same striking pattern as the clear, drive and smash shots.

Employ a soft deceptive "touch" to the shuttle.

Contact the shuttle at its highest possible trajectory.

An overhead should be contacted slightly in front of body plane and to the side to assure a soft downward trajectory.

Use less wrist action and slow the racket head at the point of contact.

Employ the drop shot if you are out of position and need time to recover or if you want to lure the opponent out of center court position.

An effective drop shot should land within three feet or one meter from the opponent's net.

Practice Techniques

Partner sets up high clears and you strike shuttle using varied drop striking patterns. Partner permits the shuttle to hit ground and provides you with feedback concerning deception and placement accuracy. Repeat.

Rally high clears and drops.

Rally drops and hairpins.

Rally cross court hairpins.

Common Errors

Racket face too open on overhead drop shot.

Too much wrist snap—resulting in set up to the opponent.

No deception!

Push instead of hitting with soft "touch" and follow through.

Shuttlecock flight common errors

Shuttle going up instead of down on overhead drop shot—playing shuttle behind body, racket face too open.

Too hard—too much wrist and arm snap.

Going too deep—same errors and racket face too open.

Creative Tips

Place standards next to the court with a white wire in the shape of a hairpin (bendable) to show visually the flight path of a hairpin drop shot.

Place strings across the net at various heights. Attempt to keep shuttle between the lowest strings to attain the highest point values.

Place targets or boxes next to the net to hit drop shots in. The closer to the net, the higher the point value.

Practice altering shuttle so that it travels slower to obtain a hairpin trajectory.

For overhead drop, tape the racket handle to your hand so that the racket face remains closed in order to hit the shuttle consistently downward (Figure 7.4).

Figure 7.4. An example of a taped racket.

53

Thought Provoker

"Rhyme Time"

Fill in the blank with a word that rhymes with the italicized word in the sentence.

1. When one looks *around* the shuttle is found going _____ on the overhead drop.

2. With overhead drop shots a *misconception* is that they look different than other shots but really the key is _____ .

3. Overhead drops they say with a smile should be *short* and be hit from the back of the _____ .

4. The hairpin that goes high can be easily smashed to a *mist* when the basic problem is more than likely in the _____ .

5. It is anyone's *bet* but both hairpins and overhead drops should be hit close to the _____ .

6. Some people give a relief in the form of a *sigh* but in an effective overhead drop the shuttle is contacted _____ .

The Smash

8

The smash is the ultimate power shot and the strongest offensive shot in badminton. It is the shot that may kill or put away the opponent. The smash may be hit from either the forehand or the backhand side. Some players prefer to employ the round-the-head smash if the shuttle must be struck from a backhand overhead position. Usually the smash is hit off of a poor clear so there is time to move around a backhand shot and play it with the forehand. The striking pattern and the basic fundamentals of the smash are similar to that of other overhead forehand and backhand shots such as the clear and drop. The smash, however, differs from the clear or drop shot in that at the point of contact with the shuttle the face of the racket head is approximately at a 45° angle with the playing surface. The face is closed and contact is made to the side and slightly forward of the body plane. (Figures 8.1–8.5) A strong forearm and wrist action propel the shuttle at this angle straight toward the floor. The further from the net the attacking player attempts the smash shot, the more time the opponent will have to react to the shuttle and the less the downward angle of the shuttle. The smash shot should be employed when the shuttle is at a proper height and in the front two thirds of the court (front half for beginners). The smash should be powerful and directed toward the open court area. Occasionally, if the opponent is in proper court position the smash is directed slightly to the right of the midline of the opponent's body. This is called a body smash and is difficult for the opponent to return because the racket head is usually positioned to the left side of the midline of the body in the ready position. Proper placement of the body smash makes it very difficult for the opponent to react in order to make a return.

One drawback of the smash is that it leaves the attacking player off balance and vulnerable, especially if the opponent counters the attacking player's smash with a blocking shot. To prevent this off balance position after a smash is hit, some players employ the half smash. The half smash is a smash hit with less body movement allowing the attacking player to maintain the proper balance necessary to recover and return to proper center court position. The half smash travels at about 75% maximum shuttle speed and is usually not classified as a clear cut winning shot like

Figure 8.1   **Figure 8.2**   **Figure 8.3**

Figure 8.4   **Figure 8.5**

Figures 8.1–8.5. The overhead smash shot.

the full smash. Nevertheless, the half smash forces the opponent to apply a defensive underhand stroking pattern for the return which enables the attacking player to keep the opponent on the defense as well as enabling the attacking player to maintain proper court posture. Properly hit, the smash can result in a clear cut and satisfying winning shot which all players should strive to perform effectively and efficiently.

Suggestions Concerning the Smash

Reach as high as possible for the shuttle.

Contact the shuttle in front of the body.

Maintain proper body balance while smashing.

Don't over hit the smash. Power is important but the accuracy and pace of the smash are to be controlled.

Do not attempt a smash if you are out of position and off balance.
Keep racket face closed.
Don't overuse the smash.

Practice Techniques

Partner hits short high clear to you between net and service line and you smash it.
Hit both medium high and high sets—beginners are more successful with a medium high set. Let your partner smash successfully. Accuracy in the set up is important!
Rally the shuttle back and forth with different shots using the smash and half smash where appropriate.
Same as drill number one except increase the depth of the clear as you become more proficient at smashing.

Common Errors

Not watching the shuttle.
Body not sideways.
Hitting the shuttle passively.
Hitting the shuttle too far behind the body (open racket face).
Hitting it too deep in your court to be effective; a good player will return your smash usually with a winning dropshot.
Not relaxing the arm.

Shuttlecock fight common errors

Too deep or out of court past baseline—hitting the shuttle behind you or your racket face is too open.
Lack of power—wrist snap, follow through, windup, step body position and rotation may be suspect!

Creative Tips

Employ a shuttle that goes at higher speeds than a normal shuttle. This can be accomplished by clipping the plastic feathers, tipping them inward or placing a rubberband loosely around the feathers.
Smash from high area. Place mats in a pile two to three feet high. Practice smashing down from this elevated area to show effectiveness of high contact. (Figures 8.6–8.8)
Place a small dangling stationary shuttle on a rubberband or string and hang it high. Force the student to reach up to hit it until it releases from the string.
Shadow drills with students mimicking the instructor. All students should face the instructor as the smash technique is broken down into integral components. Emphasize the reach and proper racket face contact with the shuttle.

Figure 8.6   **Figure 8.7**   **Figure 8.8**

Figures 8.6–8.8. Smash shot from an elevated position.

Thought Provoker

Take each group of letters and rearrange them into key concepts related to the smash.

Word   *Key Concept*

1. W O D N   _____

2. A D R H   _____

3. L L T E H A   _____

4. O E P R W   _____

5. T F N'O R   R O C U T   _____

6. L F H A   M S S A H   _____

7. V E E N F O F I S   _____

8. I H H G   R L E C A   _____

9. T R U G N   _____

10. D R E F A H O N   _____

The Round-the-Head Shot

9

The round-the-head shot is an overhead forehand shot that is employed when the shuttle is on the backhand side of the player. The round-the-head shot is often used by players who possess a weak backhand overhead shot and prefer to use the more powerful forehand striking pattern. (Figures 9.1 and 9.2) The round-the-head shot may result in a clear, drive, smash, half smash or drop shot depending on the court position of the opponent and the shuttle to be played. The striking pattern of the round-the-head shot is similar to that of the forehand overhead striking pattern. The major difference is that the point of contact with the shuttle is over the left shoulder area instead of the right shoulder of the player. In order to strike the shuttle over the left shoulder, the racket arm is partially flexed as the arm reaches upward and backward in a circular fashion around the head. As the arm moves in its circular path the trunk and body will hyperextend or arch backward and the racket arm will reach across the head in order to make contact with the shuttle. Upon contact with the shuttle the shoulders will be parallel with the net as will the palm of the right hand and the weight will be on the left foot. Because of this body and racket arm action most round-the-head shots are directed straight ahead rather than cross court. The major drawback of employing the round-the-head shot is that it causes the player to lean to the backhand side of the court, leaving the player's forehand side of the court open for an effective return by the opponent. It is, therefore, critical to return to the center court position as quickly as possible after striking an effective round-the-head placement or to put the shuttle away without the opponent returning the shot. In doubles especially if the side-by-side strategy is being employed, the "leaning" effect has less draw back since the players court coverage responsibilities permit coordination of effort for returning the shuttle.

Suggestions Concerning the Round-the-Head Shot

Be sure to move to the proper striking position.
Contact the shuttle over the left shoulder.
Be deceptive! The clear, drive, drop, smash and half smash should look the same.
Be sure to return to proper court position as the forehand court is vulnerable to an effective return.

Figure 9.1. The around-the-head clear shot.

Figure 9.2. The around-the-head drop or smash shot.

Practice Techniques

Same as other skill shots but played with round-the-head striking pattern.

Common Errors

Not being deceptive.
Not taking racket through a full circular range of motion.
Not keeping your balance.

Creative Tips

Place circles on the net and court with tape to remind the player to concentrate on a circular action striking pattern. (Figure 9.3)

Make a cardboard halo and attach to a hat so that it is a few inches above the player's head. The player should copy the circular halo pattern with the path of the arm and racket when practicing the round-the-head striking pattern.

Figure 9.3. Circled net visual aid.

Thought Provoker

Take the following paragraph and relate it to the round-the-head shot.

An automobile engine is a highly sophisticated technological machine. It permits humankind to transport themselves and materials from one location to another with little effort, rather than walking and hand carrying the materials. There are many components in an automobile engine that must work together in order for the engine to perform to maximum capacity. The functioning of the engine is directly related to the working of its parts.

The Net Shots

10

The label net shot is given to any number of short shot selections which are initiated between the net and the short service line. The clear, drop and smash shot fall into this category and become the underhand clear, the underhand net drop, including the hairpin drop, the dump shot (variations including the flick, jab, tumbler and spinner) and the net smash and half smash. Each of these respective shot's striking patterns and basic fundamentals have been discussed in previous sections. The net shot may be employed to attempt to put away the opponent as with the net smash or to keep the opponent off balance and out of proper center court position as with the net drop shot selections. It is important to note that the attacking player may not reach over the net or hit the net with the racket or body when attempting to make contact with the shuttle. The racket, however, may break the plane of the net on the follow through.

Another net shot that has not been discussed is the push shot. The push shot is employed primarily in doubles competition when the opponents are positioned in an up-and-back formation. The push shot may be struck by either the forehand or the backhand and it requires the shuttle to be contacted above the top of the net. The object of the push shot is to softly push the shuttle past the up opponent who is positioned in the front court and in front and to the side of the back opponent. The flight pattern of the push shot is illustrated in Figure 3.23 and usually terminates in the midcourt area. In this way the push shot is similar to the midcourt drive except that contact is made closer to the net and less force is needed to propel the shuttle to its midcourt destination. The flight pattern of the shuttle should require the opponent to employ a defensive underhand striking pattern or pop-up for the return. Variations of the push shot include the brush and dab shots whose descriptions are self explanatory. The dump shot and its variations is still another net shot used when returning an opponent's weak return or low serve. As the shuttle crosses the net, it is struck with the racket face parallel to the floor and guided back over the net (Figures 10.1–10.3). If the return is hard driven, a simple block will often suffice or a touch and give shot, absorbing the force of the shuttle, will allow you to dump the shuttle into the opponent's court. If the oncoming shuttle falls below the net then a hairpin shot which was discussed in Chapter 7 may be employed.

| Figure 10.1 | Figure 10.2 | Figure 10.3 |

Figures 10.1–10.3. The return of a soft shot using the dump.

Most net shots require touch, finesse, quickness, precision, and some deception in order to be effective. The execution of the net shot usually leaves little margin for error. The net shot is a vital component of the game of badminton, and if struck properly can lead to a weak return by the opponent allowing you to take over control of the play and prescribe the next shot.

Suggestions Concerning the Net Shots

Contact the shuttle in as high a position as possible.

Strike the shuttle with a light touch in order to place the shuttle close to the opponent's side of the net.

An abbreviated backswing may be necessary.

Place the shuttle as close to the opponent's side of the net as possible except on the underhand clear and push shot.

The lower the point of contact with the shuttle in relation to the net the more difficult the returning net shot.

Practice Techniques

Partner hits high (poor) drop shots—hit your repertoire of net shots.

Partner hits medium smashes—hit your repertoire of net shots.

Partner hits high hairpins—hit your repertoire of net shots.

Partner hits drives—hit your repertoire of net shots.

Common Errors

Not enough force imparted on slow returns.
Too much force imparted on hard driven returns.
Not reacting with the racket quickly enough.
Hitting a defensive rather than an offensive shot.

Creative Tips

Hit with a larger racket face (over-sized tennis racket).
Use a shorter handled racket (racketball).
Tape elbows to your side to remind you to keep the elbows close to the body for quicker racket movement.

Thought Provoker

Describe net shots using the analogies indicated below.

1. Swatting a fly with a fly swatter when the fly is resting on a fragile item.
   Description—

2. Catching a tennis ball thrown hard by hand.
   Description—

3. Lifting a heavy object which is balanced on one hand to a shelf above the head.
   Description—

4. Snapping the fingers.
   Description—

The Development of a Complete Badminton Player

Suggestions Concerning Court Sense
Practice Techniques
Related Conditioning Practices
Thought Provoker

11

Two of the key components of developing into a complete badminton player are court sense and practice technique. In order to become a complete player, the participant must develop the basic knowledge and understanding of what to do on the badminton court. Knowing what shot to employ and where to place the shot selection are vital components of successful play. To be effective, the player should correctly strike the shuttle to the appropriate court position a high percentage of the time. Developing this quality requires time, effort and proper practice technique. There is little substitute for actual match play with players of equal or greater skill and experience in order to acquire the motivation for learning what to do and when to do it in regard to the conduct of the game of badminton. More important, however, for the complete badminton player, is to be able to select the appropriate shot selection and to be able to confidently and successfully hit the shot a high percentage of the time. These are not easy tasks to master, but these are the vital ingredients which constitute the complete player. It is these attributes that all players, regardless of the level of play should strive to accomplish to some desired degree of effectiveness.

The first part of this section will deal primarily with court sense suggestions on what to do when involved in the game of badminton. These suggestions will serve as a foundation for development of court sense and sound judgment in regard to the conduct of the game of badminton. The second part of the section will deal with some self-evaluative techniques of practice. Participation in these self evaluative skill drills will assist the player in developing the necessary repertoire of badminton fundamentals in order to become a complete player. These practice techniques or skill drills will emphasize such fundamentals as conditioning, concentration, coordination, quickness, strength, timing, agility and footwork as applied to the fundamental shots of badminton. The suggestions presented concerning the practice techniques or skill drills are not meant to be a rigid or exhaustive list. The suggestions, it is hoped, will serve as a guide for each individual player to develop his or her own individualized package of practice techniques which will meet each player's specific needs and desired goals. The third section will deal with some suggestions concerning conditioning, which is thought to be requisite to becoming a complete badminton player.

Suggestions Concerning Court Sense

Knowing how to react and where to be on the badminton court during play is a complex task. Below are a list of general guidelines which may assist the player in developing sound court sense and judgment during play.

Always maintain the ready position, which is a position of physical and mental awareness. Be relaxed but ready and do not grip the racket too tightly.

Attempt to maintain proper center court position at all times. The player may wish to take a step or two toward the side line to which the shuttle is placed in order to maintain the proper center court position.

Try to force the opponent to move either forward or backward and out of center court position. A series of clear and drop shots may be used to accomplish this goal.

When serving in singles, employ the high deep serve to the backhand corner of the receiver's court a majority of the time. This serve should move the opponent out of center court position.

When serving in doubles, employ the low short serve or flick serve to the center of the court as the court length is shortened compared to singles.

The striking angle for the return is also reduced by placing the shuttle in the center of the court.

When receiving service in singles, protect the backhand side by assuming a position near the center line when in the right service court and in the left middle of the court when in the left service court. Do not stand too far back in the service court as there is ample time for the player to move backwards to receive a high deep serve and less time to move forward to receive the low short serve.

When receiving a low short serve in doubles, the receiver should attempt to return either a dump or push shot to the midcourt area.

When receiving an effective high deep serve or clear, one of the most effective and safest returns is a high deep clear to the rear and center of the opponent's court.

During play get to the shuttle as soon as possible in order to make contact at the highest point.

Do not overrun the shuttle as this will make it difficult for the player to return to proper center court position as well as cause the player to be off balance when contacting the shuttle.

Remain in the ready position until the shuttle is struck by the opponent. The player, however, should mentally calculate the most probable return by the opponent and be ready for it. Anticipation is important but do not react too soon.

Keep your eye on the shuttle when striking it. Concentration is vital!

Pace yourself. The player should control the tempo and flow of the game. Be patient and don't become reckless.

Do not over hit the shuttle. Players frequently over smash without putting away the shuttle.

Maintain a court coolness and do not overtly react to the opponent, spectators or umpire.

When returning a smash in singles play, attempt to block the shuttle and drop the shuttle over the net to the farthest point away from the opponent.

Do not give away early points. Play every point like a match point.

If in doubt whether to play a shuttle that may be close to being out of play, play the shuttle if the opponent has served, because a point is at stake.

If you are going to gamble or experiment and strike a low percentage shot, do it on your service as you will not lose a point and may in fact gain one.

When the opponent is effectively hitting cross court drop and net shots, return the shuttle deep and to the center of the court. This will reduce the opponent's striking angle of return.

The player who employs the round-the-head shot often leaves the forehand side open to an effective return.

Attempt to establish what the opponent's strengths and weaknesses are and play them to your advantage.

Play conservatively in the beginning of the game as the opponent may make a series of unforced errors and place himself or herself in a predicament.

During doubles play, attempt not to hit cross court service returns or smash shots or the opponent playing at the net may block them effectively. Try to drop, drive, push or half smash down the closest side line or straight ahead. If you want to stabilize your game and minimize unforced errors, hit to the center of the opponent's court. Also, whenever the opponent serves, avoid giving up a point on an unforced error. Let the opponent make the unforced error!

Doubles is a game hitting down, play mostly drops, smashes and drives.

In most circumstances, attempt to hit the shuttle away from the opponent.

When opponent is back, use hairpins, drops and smashes.

When opponent is up, employ pushes, attacking clears and drives.

Vary your game to keep your opponent off balance.

Practice Techniques

The following series of skill drills will enable the player to practice the various important components of the game of badminton. The suggested skill drills are certainly not meant to be a complete list, but may serve as a model for each player to develop his or her own set of practice routines which will enable the player to further develop the skill and stamina to become a complete player.

Down the Line — Cross Court Overhead Clear

The drill begins with a deep high singles serve to the forehand side of the receiver. The service return is placed down the closest side line with a forehand overhead clear shot. The shuttle is then placed cross court by the original server and played again down the closest sideline by the receiver using either forehand, backhand or round-the-head overhead clear shots. The server will always be hitting cross court shots and the receiver will always be striking the shuttle down the closest side line. The players should exchange roles after each has contacted the shuttle 20 times. This drill will help develop stamina and lateral footwork as well as the forehand, backhand and round-the-head overhead clear shots. (Figure 11.1)

Overhead Drop Shot and Underhand Clear

The drill begins with a deep high singles serve to the forehand side of the server. The service return is an overhead drop shot placed to the center of the court and close to the net of the server. The shuttle is then cleared by the original server using an underhand clear shot. This clear shot is once again returned by employing an overhead drop shot and this playing pattern should continue until each player strikes the shuttle 20 times. The shuttle should be placed to both the forehand and backhand sides of each player. The players should then switch roles so that each one receives the opportunity to practice each of the techniques required to strike an overhead drop and underhand clear shot. This drill will help develop stamina, forward and backward footwork as well as a deceptive forehand and backhand underhand net clear. The forehand, backhand and round-the-head overhead drop shots will also be developed. Each of the striking patterns of the overhead shots should be disguised to resemble that of the overhead clear shot. (Figure 11.2)

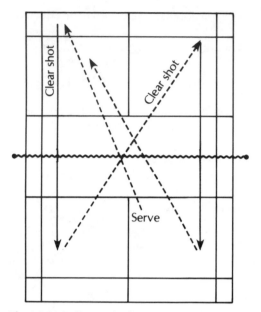

Figure 11.1. Down the line — cross court overhead clear.

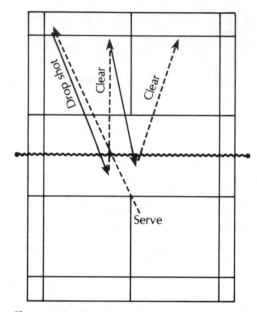

Figure 11.2. Overhead drop shot and underhand clear.

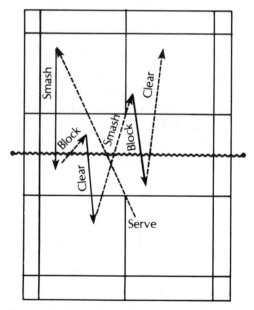

Figure 11.3. Smash, drop underhand clear, smash drill.

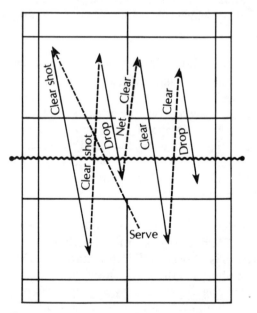

Figure 11.4. Alternating clear and drop combination drill (AC-DC Drill).

Smash, Drop, Underhand Clear, Smash Drill

The drill begins with a medium high singles serve to the forehand side of the receiver. The serve is smashed straight ahead by the receiver. The server then blocks the smash attempting to drop the shuttle to the center of the court and close to the original receiver's net. The receiver then employs an underhand net clear shot to the midcourt area of the server. The original server then smashes this midcourt clear and this playing pattern is repeated. This drill should be practiced until each player contacts the shuttle 20 consecutive times. This drill will help develop stamina, footwork, reaction time and concentration as well as the overhead forehand, backhand, round-the-head smash shots and half smash shots. The skill and technique of blocking and dropping the smash and the forehand and backhand underhand net clear are also practiced under pressure conditions. (Figure 11.3)

Alternating Clear and Drop Combination Drill (AC-DC Drill)

The drill begins with a deep high singles serve to the forehand side of the receiver. The service return is an overhand clear shot placed deep and to the center of the server's court. The server will return with an overhead clear shot to the midcourt of the original receiver's court. The receiver, using the identical overhead striking pattern this time will drop the shuttle instead of hitting a deep high clear. The receiver will then alternate hitting overhead clear and overhead drop shots while the server will always be employing an underhand net clear or overhead high clear to set up the receiver's alternating overhead clear and drop shots. The players should exchange roles after each has contacted the shuttle 20 times. The shuttle may also be moved to both the forehand and backhand sides as the players become proficient at the practice technique. This drill will help the player develop a deceptive overhead drop shot as well as develop a powerful high deep clear. (Figure 11.4)

Drive Drill

The drill begins with a medium high singles serve to the forehand side of the receiver. The service return is driven down the closest sideline. The shuttle is then driven cross court by the original server and played again down the closest sideline by the receiver using a combination of forehand and backhand fast drive and midcourt drive shots. The server will always be hitting cross court drives and the receiver will always be striking the shuttle down the closest sideline. The players should exchange roles after each has contacted the shuttle 20 times. This drill will help develop stamina, footwork, reaction time and concentration as well as all variations of the drive shot technique and is initiated similar to Figure 11.1.

The Service Square Drill

The serve, although not considered an offensive stroke, is still one of the most important shots in the game of badminton. For this reason, the serve should be practiced until it becomes an effective part of every player's game. To practice the serve, gather 20 shuttles and assume the proper service position. Then, without alternating service courts, serve five shuttles in succession into each of the four preferred singles service placement areas as shown in Figure 11.5. Then switch to the left service court and repeat the same practice pattern. The appropriate double serves may be practiced in the same manner. This drill will help develop the skill, finesse and consistency necessary to be an effective server.

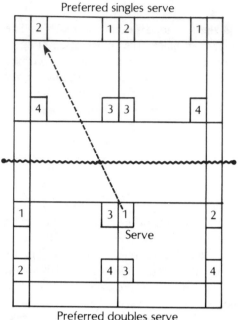

Preferred singles serve

Serve

Preferred doubles serve

Figure 11.5. Preferred singles and doubles service placement "sweet spots" for implementation and assessment of the Service Square Drill.

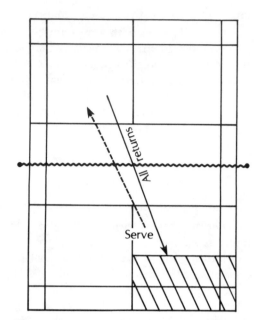

All returns

Serve

Figure 11.6. Pre-D drill with receiver hitting to striped or designated area.

Pre D Drill

The drill begins with a medium high serve to the receiver's forehand. The receiver is restricted to place the shuttle to a predetermined area on the server's side of the court such as the back one third of the right service area of the doubles court. The receiver may use any appropriate badminton shot but must place the shuttle to the predetermined area of the court. There is no restriction placed on the placement area or the shot selection employed by the server or predetermined player. This drill technique allows the server who is relatively stationary in the predetermined return area to rest and to concentrate on forcing the other player to move to all areas of the court. This drill is also helpful when one of the players is not at the same skill level as the other player as it involves a challenge for each of the players. Roles may be switched after each player has contacted the shuttle 20 times in succession. The drill helps develop stamina, footwork, concentration and accuracy while allowing the player to select and employ the basic shots of badminton. (Figure 11.6)

Drop and Net Shot Drill

The drill begins with the serve into the opponent's right service court. After the service is put into play each succeeding shot must be a drop or net that will fall in front of the opponent's short service line. After each player has contacted the shuttle five times, any player is free to smash the shuttle and terminate the drill. This practice technique may also be modified into an actual game situation using only drop shots, redefining the boundary lines, and playing to a set number of points. These practice techniques develop stamina, footwork, finesse and touch around the net.

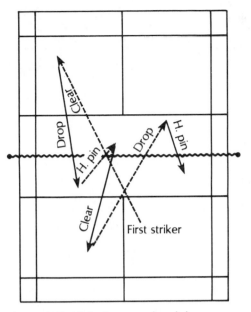
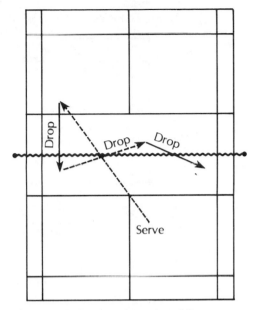

Figure 11.7. High clear, overhead drop — hairpin (H. pin) drill.

Figure 11.8. Drop and net shot drill.

High Clear, Overhead Drop — Hairpin Drill

The first striker hits a deep clear, receiver hits an overhead drop, the first striker then hits a hairpin and the receiver hits an underhand clear and the cycle continues. It helps for each player to call out the shot such as "drop", "hairpin", etc., before contacting the shuttle. This assists the partner to anticipate the upcoming shot. This is an excellent drill for up-back movement patterns and footwork practice. The drill also aids in anticipation and concentration which are both exceedingly important in the game of badminton. The more precise the shots employed in this drill, the more difficult the drill becomes. The drill is also beneficial for shot technique and skill acquisition. (Figure 11.7)

Games of Reduced Area

There are any number of games that can be conceived by reducing the area of the playing court. Games may be played just within the short singles boundary lines as mentioned in the Drop and Net Shot Drill. Half court singles, half court versus one service court, the diagonal service court, singles court versus doubles court, base line (the rear two and a half feet or .76 meter of the court) versus front court (the front six and one half feet or 1.98 meters of the court) are just a few of the many reduced area games. Reduced area games provide a challenge as well as concentrated practice in developing specific shots within a specified area of the court. Of course, the types of shots utilized by each player could also be predetermined to give the player even more specific and concentrated shot selection and placement practice. (Figure 11.8)

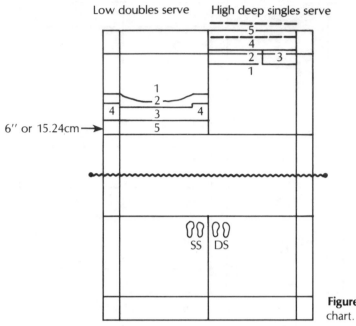

Figure 11.9. Service accuracy assessment chart.

Related Conditioning Practices

Another very important part of becoming a complete badminton player as well as an effective player is physical conditioning. It was once stated that a badminton player must have the footwork of a light weight boxing champion, the wind of a distance runner and the quickness of eye and wrist of a man fighting a bee with a popsicle (Howard, 1933). Translated this statement means that an effective player must have speed, endurance, agility, strength, flexibility and hand-eye coordination. These qualities have been alluded to in a previous section of the text. The following is a brief list of general conditioning practices that, if practiced, may improve your game of badminton.

Play. Play the game of badminton as much as possible. There seems to be little substitute for actual play to improve your game.

Run. Running certainly can increase the endurance aspect of your game.

Skipping Rope. Skipping rope is another method of developing endurance, agility and footwork.

Shuttle Throw. Throwing the shuttle across the net or against the wall may assist in developing the forehand overhead striking pattern.

Hitting Against the Wall. Hitting the shuttle against the wall or hitting the shuttle into prescribed boxes or over lines marked on a wall may help in developing the strength, coordination, accuracy and finesse of certain basic shots of badminton such as the serve and high deep clear.

Evaluation. Badminton court accuracy and power may be determined as well as developed by having the player strike the shuttle into the opponent's court in a prescribed manner. Colored yarn may be stretched across the court approximately one foot or 30.48 centimeters above the net, for example, to have the player serve under and into a numbered court as shown in Figure 11.9. The player is then able to evaluate the accuracy of the low short serve primarily

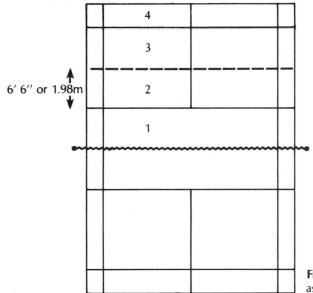

6′ 6″ or 1.98m

4

3

2

1

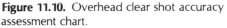

Figure 11.10. Overhead clear shot accuracy assessment chart.

used in doubles. The same yarn can be placed across the court at six feet or two meters in back of the short service line and at 9 feet or 1.98 meters in height (Figure 11.9). The high deep singles serve can then be practiced and self evaluation can take place. A scoring standard can then be developed in order to meet the needs of the player's goals and expectations. Any of the basic shots of badminton, such as the forehand and backhand overhead clear and drop shots, located in Figures 11.10 and 11.11 may be evaluated and practiced in this same manner. It is important, however, to note that the court numbering technique is just one means of positive evaluation and this method should not be employed by the instructor to exclude, eliminate or place the student-participant in a negative category. It is recommended that practice techniques such as those shown above will be used to prescribe what facets of the game of badminton the participant should work on and develop. These evaluative techniques should lead to prescriptive training techniques in order to assist each participant to achieve a certain defined standard that meets the individual needs of the participant.

For further information concerning more specific alternatives to evelation and measurement of badminton skills it is suggested that the reader consult the Badminton Bibliography and Selected Readings section of the text.

Agility. Agility drills such as the Round-the-Clock Drill can be used to develop agility, endurance, speed and flexibility. The player begins in the ready position and in the proper center court position as shown in Figure 11.12. The player then moves using the proper footwork technique to each of the numbers or shuttles placed on the court and returns to the center court before going to the next number. The player should reach out and stretch to touch the number or pick up the shuttle as the drill progresses. The drill can be timed for speed or the pace may be slowed and the practice technique used for a warm-up session.

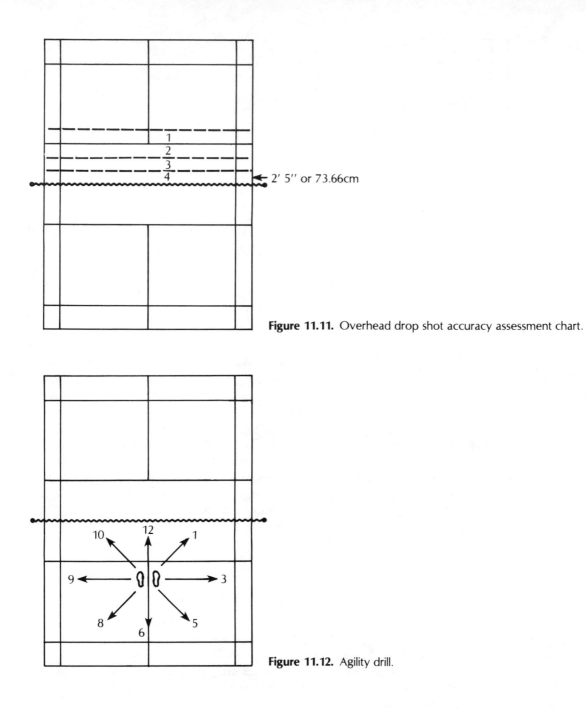

Figure 11.11. Overhead drop shot accuracy assessment chart.

2′ 5″ or 73.66cm

1
2
3
4

Figure 11.12. Agility drill.

10 12 1

9 3

8 5

6

Weight Training. Yes, weight training for badminton! Both general and specific progressive resistance weight training exercises can be designed for the serious badminton player. These exercises should be individually prescribed and may certainly assist in the development of a more powerful and forceful game. Suggested lower body, trunk, leg and forearm exercises specifically related to the game of badminton should include such exercises as forearm wrist curls, forearm reverse wrist curls, forearm wrist rotations and finger exercises for grip strength. As the badminton player develops the basic skills, a plateau will be reached where physical conditioning techniques will be sought out in order to enhance further performance. Physical conditioning including aerobic and anaerobic workout schedules are most often neglected in this process of development. Physical conditioning however is certainly a vital ingredient in becoming not only a complete badminton player but in maintaining a healthy and active quality of life. For a thorough treatment on individualized weight training and conditioning for fitness and sport it is suggested that the reader consult the weight training and conditioning references by Hatfield and Krotee (1978 and 1979) which may be found in the Badminton Bibliography and Selected Readings section of the text.

Model Forty-five Minute Badminton Workout Schedule

Duration (minutes:seconds)		Physical Activity
5:00	Warm-up	Warm-up consisting of light jogging, static stretching and light calisthenics.
5:00	Light Hitting	Utilization of your complete repertoire of badminton shots.
10:00	Specific, designed badminton skill or practice technique (i.e. overhead smash). The practice technique intensity, frequency of repetition and duration should be modified depending on the skill level, physical condition and desired outcome of the participant.	(i.e. Overhead Smash) Employ the Smash, Drop, Underhand Clear, Smash Drill. Begin with a 1:30 to 2:00 minute drill with a minute rest period between repetitions. During rest period alternate pop-up and smash accuracy drill if desired.
15:00–20:00	Game	Play game or as many points as possible.
5:00	Cooling Down Period (CDP)	Cooling down period consisting of stretching and light calisthenics.

Figure 11.13. A model badminton workout schedule. The workout schedule should be alternated and modified depending on the aims and objectives as well as the level of skill and conditioning of the participant.

Thought Provoker

1. Explain "court sense" as it applies to effective badminton competition.

2. Create a new practice drill for the—smash
                                  —drive
                                  —service

3. Draw stick figures training with weights in such a way as to benefit badminton skills.

Facilities and Equipment

12

The Nature of Facilities

The nature and spirit of the game of badminton is such that it may be played both indoors and outdoors and in almost any amount of space. Therefore, the facilities segment of this section will be very brief. Badminton has literally been played on beaches, mountain sides, and in parlors, backyards, playgrounds and national stadiums. The only necessary requirement concerning facilities seems to be enough space for safe play and subdued winds so that the shuttle is not adversely affected. Further information concerning the required space necessary for an official court, as well as for posts, nets and shuttles may be found in the section dealing with the Laws of Badminton. The power game of badminton also necessitates a buffer space surrounding the court. It is recommended that 3 feet to 5 feet or 1 to 2 meters on the sides and 10 feet or 3 meters in the back combined with a ceiling height of 24 to 30 feet or 10 meters make up an ideal and safe playing court. Ideally played indoors, proper lighting to prevent glare is requisite as is an off white ceiling so the shuttle can easily be seen from the figure-ground perspective.

Nets and Posts

Information concerning the proper size net and posts may be found in the Laws of Badminton. Proper care should be taken with the nets and posts allowing these important and expensive pieces of equipment to last for many years. Oddly enough the cost of these pieces of equipment are the most expensive of the game and may range from $7.00–$150.00 for a net and up to $150.00 for a set of long lasting posts that may be fixed to the floor of the playing surface. The net consists of the tape at the top (headband), the body or mesh part and the draw strings. Nets come in various size mesh cord (1/2 inch–1 1/2 inch) and vary in perpendicular measurements depending on cost with the heavier—larger net being more expensive.

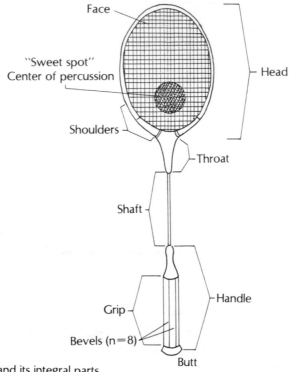

Face

"Sweet spot"
Center of percussion

Shoulders

Head

Throat

Shaft

Grip

Handle

Bevels (n=8)

Butt

Figure 12.1. The racket and its integral parts.

Racket

The laws of badminton contain specifications for the racket (Figure 12.1). Most rackets are approximately 26 inches or 660–680 mm in overall length and weigh anywhere from three and one-half (99.23 gms) to five ounces (141 gms). The racket is divided into the head, (allowable maximum width 205 m, the shaft, 11 inches (27.94cm), the grip (usually leather, gauze or towel), 5 inches (12.70 cm) and the base which is called the butt. Standard grip size ranges from 3 1/2 inches–4 1/2 inches. The face of the racket consists of the string portion and the complete racket minus strings is called the frame. Today's rackets are constructed from a myriad of materials including: steel alloys, stainless steel, aluminum, fiberglass, graphite, carbon fiber, ash, cherry, beech and hickory wood. The racket frame is usually strung with varied grades of sheep gut, nylon or linen strings. In brief it seems that the metal racket strung with nylon, resists warping and has a longer life than most inexpensive wooden rackets (Figure 12.2). Most wood rackets should be placed in a press to prevent warping. It has been found that laminated or layered wood rackets seem to resist warping better than rackets constructed from a single piece of wood. The string holes for metal rackets should have plastic grommets in the holes to protect the strings. In wooden rackets the holes should be beveled. When properly strung, the player should be able to strum the strings like a guitar and a "singing" resonance should be audible. The price of racket frames and stringing range from approximately $7.00–$65.00. The lightweight metal racket strung with nylon seems to be the most popular racket for the typical player and lies well within the price range mentioned above (Figure 12.3).

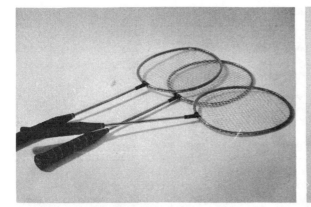

Figure 12.2. Sample metal rackets.

Figure 12.3. Examples of metal and wood rackets.

Figure 12.4. Examples of synthetic and goose feather shuttles.

Shuttle

The shuttles used in badminton have certainly come a long way from the clipped chicken feathers used to make shuttles up to the early 1900's. In 1902 the shuttle received its barrel shape and was first used in the All-England Championships. Today the average shuttle weighs less than a fifth of an ounce or 73–85 grains (4.73–5.50 grams). The cork base is about one inch (25 mm) in diameter. The principal materials used to construct the modern shuttle include: cork, fine leather, cotton, adhesive and 14 to 16 goose wing feathers. Shuttles are classified as fast (red), medium (blue), or slow (green) on the basis of the distance they fly. This factor is termed "speed" and varies with minor differences in the weight of the shuttle (the heavier the slower) as well as atmospheric conditions.

Today the synthetic or one piece nylon plastic shuttle has replaced the goose feathered shuttle for most recreational play. (Figure 12.4) In fact, names such as "Zytel" ST 810 plastic nylon resin have been scientifically developed and are being tested and shortly may replace the conventional form of nylon shuttle (Dupont, 1977). Nylon shuttles come by the dozen in a protective tube (humidity) in both outdoor and indoor varieties with the outdoor shuttle being heavier in order to be more stable in wind. The United States Badminton Association has approved such brands as Carlton and RSL for indoor tournament play and Law 4 of the Laws of Badminton defines the standards to be met if a shuttle is to be considered of correct pace and flight.

Badminton Equipment and Companies

Comfortable and light weight clothing is highly recommended for the fast moving sport of badminton including shorts and short sleeve shirt so as not to impede movement patterns. Due to the intense stop and go action of badminton, footwear, including sportshoes and socks, is very important and should be selected with care.

The following is a list of companies that can provide the reader with more information concerning the products utilized to participate in the game of badminton.

Selected Badminton Equipment and Sports Companies*

Albany International Corps
Portable Surface Department
P.O. Box 1109
Albany, New York 12201

Ashaway Line and Twine Company
Ashaway, Rhode Island 02804

Bretzke Sports
6057 East Maple
Grand Blanc, Michigan 49439

Dayton Racket Company
Arcanum, Ohio 45304

EST International Sports
Koll Business Park Building 3
2683 151st Place Northwest
Redmond, Washington 98052

Frontier Pro Shops
2750 Midway Drive
San Diego, California 92110

General Sportcraft Company, Ltd.
140 Woodbine St.
Bergenfield, New Jersey 07621

Gopher Athletic Supply Company
Highway 45N
Owatonna, Minnesota 55060

HCP Badminton Supplies
8577 Telfair Street
Sun Valley, California 91352

Carlton Sports Co., Ltd.
Shire Hill
Saffron Walden
Essex, England

International Sports
P.O. Box 883
Hawthorne, California 90250

Louisville Badminton Supply
9411 Westport Rd. Westport Plaza
Louisville, Kentucky 40222

Gleever Sports Equipment
1010 Walnut Avenue
Des Plaines, Illinois 60016

R. S. L. Shuttlecock Co., Ltd.
P.O. Box 649
Altoona, Pennsylvania 16603

Racquets International
P.O. Box 90203
World Way Postal Center
Los Angeles, California 90009

Rocky Mountain Racket and Sports
Equipment
P.O. Box 739
Loveland, Colorado 80537

S. J. Sporting Products Ltd.
Rose Place
Liverpool L3 3HS
England

Sportland
8102 La Mesa Boulevard
La Mesa, California 92041

Sports Pal Company, Inc.
P.O. Box 28906
St. Louis, Missouri 63132

Gold Country
421 14th Ave. SE
Minneapolis, MN 55414

*It is always recommended that you deal directly with your local sport shop when selecting equipment.

Badminton Budget

Racket	$10.00–25.00	Sport Clothes	$40.00
Racket Press	$ 6.00	Head and Sweat Band	$ 4.00
Shuttles	$10.00–15.00/dozen	Badminton Net	$15.00–150.00
Racket Cover	$ 3.50	Posts and Standards	$15.00–150.00
Stringing (aylew/gut)	$ 5.00–20.00	Racket Carrying Bag	$25.00
Badminton Fleece Balls	$10.00/dozen		

There are many product lines available from which the player may select the above equipment. The following, although not a complete listing, gives the reader an idea of corporate diversification.

Rackets	*Strings*	*Shuttles*	*Nets*
Bancroft	Ashway	Carlton	Coast Marketing Group
Black Knight	Ballco	Champion	Sportcraft
Carlton	Bow	EST International	Victory
Dunhill	Brand	Manta	
Dunlop	Leonia	Regent	
Grays	Victor	Rackets International	
Kawasaki	Yonex	RSC	
Kennex		Sportcraft	
Vicort		Victor	
Yonex		Wilson	
Slazenger		H. L. International	
Sportcraft		Dupont	
Sugiyama			

Thought Provoker

Circle whether the statements are True or False (T or F) and indicate why?

1. Badminton racket frames are made exclusively of wood.   T   F   Why?

2. Nylon shuttlecocks are more appropriately used by beginners than feathered shuttlecocks.
   T   F   Why?

3. There are very few badminton equipment suppliers in the United States. T   F   Why?

4. All badminton nets are basically the same.   T   F   Why?

5. A 21' high ceiling is appropriate for badminton.   T   F   Why?

6. Jeans and a loose fitting shirt is the basic clothing to be worn in playing badminton.
   T   F   Why?

7. There is no "Law of Badminton" that regulates racket size.   T   F   Why?

8. All shuttles are standard concerning size and speed.   T   F   Why?

The Laws of Badminton (United States Badminton Association)

Interpretations
Match Scheduling
The Draw
Scoring Systems
Thought Provoker

13

The laws of badminton may change slightly from year to year, hence to assure yourself that you are operating under the most current rules you can secure them from the following address:

United States Badminton Association
P.O. Box 456
Waterford, MI 48095
313-655-4502

1. COURT—a) The court shall be laid out as in Figure 13.1 (except in the case provided for in paragraph "b" of this Law) and to the measurements there shown, and shall be defined preferably by white or yellow lines, or, if this is not possible, by other easily distinguishable line, 1½ inches (40 mm) wide.

   In marking the court, the width (1½ inches or 40 mm) of the center lines shall be equally divided between the right and left service-courts; the width (1½ inches or 40 mm each) of the short service line and the long service line shall fall within the 13-foot (3.96 meters) measurement given as the length of the service-court; and the width (1½ inches or 40 mm each) of all other boundary lines shall fall with the measurements given.

   b) Where space does not permit of the marking out of a court for doubles, a court may be marked out for singles only as shown in Figure 13.2. The back boundary lines become also the long service lines, and the posts, or the strips of material representing them as referred to in Law 2, shall be placed on the side lines.

   c) The height of a court for international competitive play shall be a minimum of 30 feet or 9 meters from the floor over the full court. This height shall be entirely free of girders and other obstructions over the area of the court.

   There shall also be at least 4 feet or 1.25 meters clear space surrounding all the outer lines of the court, this space being also a minimum requirement between any two courts marked out side by side.

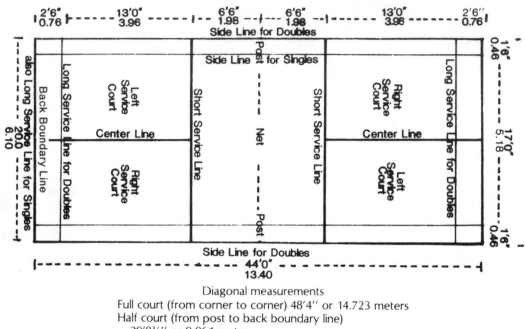

Diagonal measurements
Full court (from corner to corner) 48'4'' or 14.723 meters
Half court (from post to back boundary line)
29'8¾'' or 9.061 meters

Figure 13.1. Singles and doubles court.

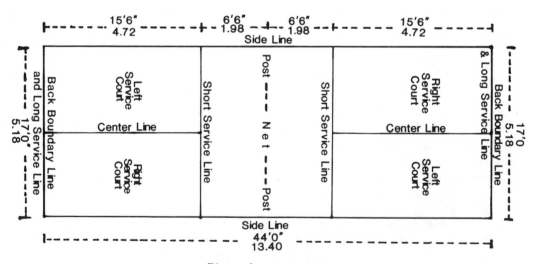

Diagonal measurements
Full court (from corner to corner) 47'2'' or 14.366 meters
Half court (from post to back boundary line) 27'9⅝'' or 8.469 meters

Figure 13.2. Singles court.

2. POSTS—The posts shall be 5 feet 1 inch (1.55 meters) in height from the surface of the court. They shall be sufficiently firm to keep the net strained as provided in Law 3, and shall be placed on the side boundary lines of the court. Where this is not practicable, some method must be employed for indicating the position of the side boundary line where it passes under the net, e.g., by the use of a thin post or strip of material, not less than 1½ inches (40 mm) in width, fixed to the side boundary line and rising vertically to the net cord. Where this is in use on a court marked for doubles it shall be placed on the side boundary line of the doubles court irrespective of whether singles or doubles are being played.

3. NET—The net shall be made of fine natural cord or artificial fiber of a dark color and an even thickness not exceeding ⅝ inch to ¾ inch (1.5 to 2 cm) mesh. It shall be firmly stretched from post to post, and shall be 2 feet 6 inches (.76 meters) in depth. The top of the net shall be 5 feet (1.524 meters) in height from the floor at the center, and 5 feet 1 inch (1.55 meters) at the posts, and shall be edged with a 3-inch (7.62cm) white tape doubled and supported by a cord or cable run through the tape and strained over and flush with the top of the posts.

4. SHUTTLE—A shuttle shall weigh from 73 to 85 grains (4.73 to 5.5 grams), and shall have from 14 to 16 feathers fixed in a cork, 1 inch to 1⅛ inches (.025 to .028 meters) in diameter. The feathers shall be from 2½ to 2¾ inches (.064 to .02 meters) in length from the tip to the top of the cork base. They shall have from 2⅛ to 2½ inches (.054 to .064 meters) spread at the top and shall be firmly fastened with thread or other suitable material.

   Subject to there being no substantial variation in the general design, pace, weight and flight of the shuttle, modifications in the above specifications may be made, subject to the approval of the National Organization concerned:
   a) in places where atmospheric conditions due either to altitude or climate, make the standard shuttle unsuitable; or
   b) if special circumstances exist which make it otherwise expedient in the interests of the game.
   (Carlton Nylon Shuttles—Tournament and International grades—and RSL Plastic Shuttles, have been approved for all tournaments except adult "Open" tournaments for which $5 sanction fee is charged; Closed and Open USA Amateur Championships; and U.S. National Junior Championships.)
   A shuttle shall be deemed to be of correct pace if, when a player of average strength strikes it with a full underhand stroke from a spot immediately above one back boundary line in a line parallel to the side lines, and at an upward angle, it falls not less than 1 foot (.30 meters), and not more than 2 feet 6 inches (.76 meters), short of the other back boundary line.

5. PLAYERS—a) The word "Player" applies to all those taking part in a game. b) The game shall be played, in the case of the doubles game, by two players a side, and in the case of the singles game, by one player a side. c) The side for the time being having the right to serve shall be called the "In" side, and the opposing side shall be called the "Out" side.

6. THE TOSS—Before commencing play the opposing sides shall toss, and the side winning the toss shall have the option of: a) serving first; or b) not serving first; or c) choosing ends. The side losing the toss shall then have choice of any alternative remaining.

7. SCORING—a) The doubles and men's singles game consists of 15 or 21 points, as may be arranged. Provided that in a game of 15 points, when the score is 13 all, the side which first reached 13 has the option of "setting" the game to 5, and that when the score is 14 all, the side which first reached 14 has the option of "setting" the game to 3. After a game has been "set" the score is called "love all" and the side which first scores 5 or 3 points, according as the game has been "set" at 13 or 14 all, wins the game. In either case the claim to "set" the game must be made before the next service is delivered after the score has reached 13 all or 14 all. Provided also that in a game of 21 points the same method of scoring be adopted, substituting 19 and 20 for 13 and 14. (In all Championship play, 15 points is the official game, rather than 21.)

    b) The ladies' single game consists of 11 points. Provided that when the score is "9 all" the player who first reached 9 has the option of "setting" the game to 2.

    c) A side rejecting the option of "setting" at the first opportunity shall not thereby be debarred from "setting" if a second opportunity arises.

    d) In handicap games "setting" is not permitted.

8. The opposing sides shall contest the best of 3 games, unless otherwise agreed. The players shall change ends at the commencement of the second game and also of the third game (if any). In the third game the players shall change ends when the leading score reaches:

    a) 8 in a game of 15 points;

    b) 6 in a game of 11 points;

    c) 11 in a game of 21 points;

or, in handicap events, when one of the sides has scored half the total number of points required to win the game (the next highest number being taken in case of fractions). When it has been agreed to play only one game the players shall change ends as provided above for the third game.

    If, inadvertently, the players omit to change ends as provided in this Law at the score indicated, the ends shall be changed immediately after the mistake is discovered, and the existing score shall stand.

9. DOUBLES PLAY—a) It having been decided which side is to have the first service, the player in the right-hand service-court of that side commences the game by serving to the player in the service-court diagonally opposite. If the latter player returns the shuttle before it touches the ground, it is to be returned by one of the "In" side, and then returned by one of the "Out" side, and so on, till a fault is made or the shuttle ceases to be "in play." If a fault is made by the "In" side, its right to continue serving is lost, as only one player on the side beginning a game is entitled to do so (See Law 11), and the opponent in the right-hand service-court then becomes the server; but if the service is not returned, or the fault is made by the "Out" side, the "In" side scores a point. The "In" side players then change from one service-court to the other, the service now being from the left-hand service-court to the player in the service-court diagonally opposite. So long as a side remains "In," service is delivered alternately from each service-court into the one diagonally opposite, the change being made by the "In" side when, and only when, a point is added to its score.

b) The first service of a side in each inning shall be made from the right-hand service-court. A "Service" is delivered as soon as the shuttle is struck by the server's racket. The shuttle is thereafter "in play" until it touches the ground, or until a fault or "Let" occurs, or except as provided in Law 19. After the service is delivered, the server and the player served to may take up any position they choose on their side of the net, irrespective of any boundary lines.

10. The player served to may alone receive the service, but should the shuttle touch, or be struck by his or her partner the "In" side scores a point. No player may receive two consecutive services in the same game, except as provided in Law 12.

11. Only one player of the side beginning a game shall be entitled to serve in its first innings. In all subsequent innings, each partner shall have the right, and they shall serve consecutively. The side winning a game shall always serve first in the next game, but either of the winners may serve and either of the losers may receive the service.

12. If a player serves out of turn, or from the wrong service-court (owing to a mistake as to the service-court from which service is at the time being in order), and his or her side wins the rally, it shall be a "Let," provided that such "Let" be claimed and allowed or ordered by the umpire before the next succeeding service is delivered.

   If a player of the "Out" side standing in the wrong service court is prepared to receive the service when it is delivered, and his or her side wins the rally, it shall be a "Let" provided that such "Let" be claimed and allowed or ordered by the umpire, before the next succeeding service is delivered.

   If in either of the above cases the side at fault loses the rally, the mistake shall stand and the players' position shall not be corrected.

   Should a player inadvertently change sides when he or she should not do so and the mistake not be discovered until after the next succeeding service has been delivered, the mistake shall stand, and a "Let" cannot be claimed or allowed, and the players' position shall not be corrected.

13. SINGLES PLAY—In singles Laws 9 to 12 hold good except that:
   a) The players shall serve from and receive service in their respective right-hand service-courts only when the server's score is 0 or an even number of points in the game, the service being from and received in their respective left-hand service-courts when the server's score is an odd number of points. Setting does not affect this sequence.
   b) Both players shall change service-courts after each point has been scored.

14. FAULTS—A fault made by a player of the side which is "In" puts the server out; if made by a player whose side is "Out," it counts a point to the "In" side. It is a fault;
   a) If in serving, the shuttle at the instant of being struck be higher than the server's waist, or if at the instant of the shuttle being struck the shaft of the racket be not pointing in a downward direction to such an extent that the whole of the head of the racket is discernibly below the whole of the server's hand holding the racket.
   b) If, in serving, the shuttle falls into the wrong service-court, (i.e., into the one not diagonally opposite to the server), or falls short of the short service line, or beyond the long service line, or outside the side boundary lines of the service-court into which service is in order.
   c) If the server's feet are not in the service-court from which service is at the time being in order, or if the feet of the player receiving the service are not in the service-court diagonally opposite until the service is delivered. (See Law 16).

d) If before or during the delivery of the service any player makes preliminary feints or otherwise intentionally balks his or her opponent or if any player deliberately delays serving the shuttle, or in getting ready to receive it, so as to obtain an unfair advantage.

e) If, either in service or play, the shuttle falls outside the boundaries of the court, or passes through or under the net, or fails to pass the net, or touches the roof or side walls, or the person or dress of a player. (A shuttle falling on a line shall be deemed to have fallen in the court or service-court of which such line is a boundary.)

f) If the shuttle "in play" be struck before it crosses to the striker's side of the net. (The striker may, however, follow the shuttle over the net with his or her racket in the course of the stroke.)

g) If, when the shuttle is "in play," a player touches the net or its supports with racket, person or dress.

h) If the shuttle be held on the racket (i.e., caught or slung) during the execution of a stroke; or if the shuttle be hit twice in succession by the same player with two strokes; or if the shuttle be hit by a player and his partner successively.

i) If in play a player strikes the shuttle (unless he or she thereby makes a good return) or is struck by it, whether he or she is standing within or outside the boundaries of the court.

j) If a player obstructs an opponent.

k) If Law 16 be transgressed.

15. GENERAL—The server may not serve till the opponent is ready, but the opponent shall be deemed to be ready if a return of the service be attempted.

16. The server and the player served to must stand within the limits of their respective service-courts (as bounded by the short and long service, the center, and side lines), and some part of both feet of these players must remain in contact with the surface of the court in a stationary position until the service is delivered. A foot on or touching a line in the case of either the server or the receiver shall be held to be outside the service-court. (See Law 14 c). The respective partners may take up any position, provided they do not unsight or otherwise obstruct an opponent.

17. a) If, in the course of service or rally, the shuttle touches and passes over the net, the stroke is not invalidated thereby. It is a good return if the shuttle, having passed outside either post, drops on or within the boundary lines of the opposite court. A "Let" may be given by the umpire, for any unforeseen or accidental hinderance.

b) If, in service, or during a rally, a shuttle, after passing over the net, is caught in or on the net, it is a "Let".

c) If the receiver is faulted for moving before the service is delivered, or for not being within the correct service-court, in accordance with Laws 14c or 16, and at the same time the server is also faulted for a service infringement, it shall be a "Let".

d) When a "Let" occurs, the play since the last service, shall not count, and the player who served shall serve again, except when Law 12 is applicable.

18. If the server, in attempting to serve, misses the shuttle, it is not a fault; but if the shuttle be touched by the racket, a service is thereby delivered.

19. If, when in play, the shuttle strikes the net and remains suspended there, or strikes the net and falls towards the surface of the court on the striker's side of the net, or hits the surface outside the court and an opponent then touches the net or shuttle with his or her racket or person, there is no penalty, as the shuttle is not then in play.

20. If a player has a chance of striking the shuttle in a downward direction when quite near the net, the opponent must not put up his or her racket near the net on the chance of the shuttle rebounding from it. This is obstruction with the meaning of Law 14 j. A player may, however, hold up the racket to protect his or her face from being hit if the player does not thereby balk his or her opponent.

21. It shall be the duty of the umpire to call "Fault" or "Let" should either occur, without appeal being made by the players, and to give the decision on any appeal regarding a point in dispute, if made before the next service; and also to appoint linesmen and service judges at his or her discretion. The umpire's decision shall be final, but he or she shall uphold the decision of a linesman or service judge. This does not preclude the umpire also from faulting the server or receiver. Where, however, a referee is appointed, an appeal shall lie to him or her from the decision of an umpire on questions of law only.

22. CONTINUOUS PLAY—Play shall be continuous from the first service until the match be concluded: except that a) in the International Badminton Championships and in the Ladies' International Badminton Championship there shall be allowed an interval not exceeding five minutes between the second and third games of a match; b) in countries where conditions render it desirable, there shall be allowed, subject to the previously published approval of the National Organization concerned, an interval not exceeding five minutes between the second and third games of a match either singles or doubles, or both, and c) when necessitated by circumstances not within the control of the players, the umpire may suspend play for such a period as he or she may consider necessary. If play be suspended, the existing score shall stand and play be resumed from that point. Under no circumstances shall play be suspended to enable a player to recover his or her strength or wind, or to receive instruction or advice. Except in the case of an interval provided for above, no player shall be allowed to receive advice during a match or leave the court until the match be concluded without the umpire's consent. The umpire shall be the sole judge of any suspension of play and he or she shall have the right to disqualify an offender. (In the U.S., at the request of any player, a five-minute rest period between the 2nd and the 3rd game will be granted, in all events. Such a rest period is mandatory for all Junior Tournaments.)

Interpretations

1. Any movement or conduct by the server that has the effect of breaking the continuity of service after the server and receiver have taken their positions to serve and to receive the service is a preliminary feint. For example, a server who, after having taken up the position to serve, delays hitting the shuttle for so long as to be unfair to the receiver, is guilty of such conduct (see Law 14 d). Note—USA Interpretation is, it is a fault if the serve is not delivered in five seconds from the time that both server and receiver have taken their stance.
2. It is obstruction if a player invade an opponent's court with racket or person in any degree except as permitted in Law 14 f. (See Law 14 j).
3. Where necessary on account of the structure of a building, the local Badminton Authority may, subject to the right of veto of its National Organization, make by-laws dealing with cases in which a shuttle touches an obstruction.

Match Scheduling

The USBA Match Scheduling System is a procedure for "programming" a tournament so that each match in each event is scheduled at a definite time on a specific court. Control is exercised through the use of master schedules by the director of play and individual cards for each player. Each separate match is numbered which permits precise scheduling.

Details in the use of the USBA Match Scheduling System may be secured from the USBA National Office.

The Draw

1. The draw for all events at Open Tournaments shall be made in the manner set out below, and no dummy entry in singles or dummy pair in doubles may be included in the draw of any championship event. There shall be no alteration in the published draw of any championship event unless permitted under exceptional circumstances by the tournament committee, but no such alteration shall be allowed in singles events, nor in a doubles event if two or more pairs already entered should object.

   NOTE—The purpose of allowing any alteration is to enable a competitor to have a substitute partner in a doubles event if his or her original partner is prevented from playing through illness, injury, or other unavoidable hinderance. The purpose of allowing alterations is not so that any fresh entries may be introduced.

   Immediately any request for alteration is received, competitors in the event concerned shall be acquainted thereof by the Referee by means of a notice prominently displayed on the notice board (if any) and/or in the changing rooms. They shall be given reasonable time to lodge objections which shall be received in confidence.

2. Under no circumstances shall any player be permitted to enter more than once in the same event at any tournament except in double elimination tournaments.

3. In no event shall the draw be arranged, except that seeding in championship events shall be permitted under the conditions set out below.

4. The draw shall be conducted as follows:
   When the number of playing units is 4, 8, 16, 32, 64, or any higher power of 2, they shall meet in pairs in the order drawn as in the following diagram:

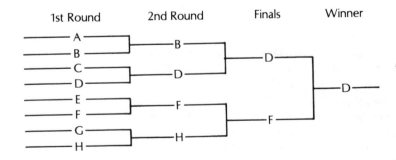

When the number of playing units is not a power of 2, there shall be byes in the first round. The number of byes shall be equal to the difference between the next highest power of 2 and the number of playing units. The byes, if even in number, shall be divided, as the names are drawn in equal proportions at the top and bottom of the list, above and below the pairs; if uneven in number, there shall be one more bye at the bottom than at the top.

Example: With 19 playing units there will be $32 - 19 = 13$ byes, 6 at the top and 7 at the bottom of the list, and 3 matches in the first round, 8 in the second, 4 in the third, etc.

Example: With 9 playing units there will be $16 - 9 = 7$ byes, 3 at the top, and 4 at the bottom, and one match in the first round; see below.

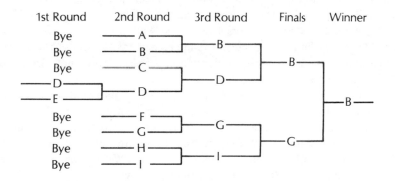

With 5 playing units there will be 1 bye at the top and 2 byes at the bottom.
With 6, 1 bye at the top and 1 bye at the bottom.
With 7, 1 bye at the bottom.
With 8, no byes.
With 9, 3 byes at the top, and 4 byes at the bottom.
With 10, 3 byes at the top, and 3 byes at the bottom.
With 11, 2 byes at the top, and 3 byes at the bottom.
With 12, 2 byes at the top, and 2 at the bottom.
With 13, 1 bye at the top, and 2 at the bottom.
With 14, 1 bye at the top, and 1 at the bottom.
With 15, 1 bye at the bottom.
With 16, no byes.

Seeding the Draw

5. At any open tournament, the draw may be arranged or "seeded" subject to the following restrictions:

   (a) Entries to the number of eight, and no more, may be seeded by lot into separate eighths of the draw of an event comprising at least 32 entries; and, similarly, in events comprising fewer entries, four may be seeded in the case of 16 or more entries, and two in the case of any smaller number, and they shall be drawn by lot into separate quarters, or halves of the draw, as the case may be.

   (b) The entries to be seeded shall be selected by the committee as being, in its opinion, the best in the event.

NOTE: For USA Tournaments other than the Open Amateur Championships the following modifications for the Seed have been approved: In case of an entry of 12 or more, but less than 16, there may be two entries placed in addition to the two seeded entries; and in the case of an entry of 24 or more, but less than 32 entries, there may be two entries placed in addition to the four seeded.

6. The seeded entries shall be drawn as follows:
   (a) If two are to be seeded, numbers 1 and 2 shall be drawn by lot; the first drawn shall be placed at the top of the upper half and the second at the bottom of the lower half.
   (b) If four are to be seeded, numbers 1 and 2 shall be placed as above; numbers 3 and 4 shall be drawn by lot and the first drawn shall be placed at the top of the second quarter; the second shall be placed at the bottom of the third quarter.
   (c) If eight are to be seeded, numbers 1, 2, 3, and 4 shall be placed as above; the remainder shall be drawn by lot and placed in the upper half, at the top of the eighths not already occupied and in the lower half, at the bottom of the eighths not already occupied. (Example on page 18.)

7. Any two entries from any country which shall be seeded shall be drawn in separate halves of the draw, and any three or four entries from any one country which shall be seeded shall be drawn in separate quarters of the draw. Note: In the United States, Regions should be considered as countries in this regard. Players from the same Region should not play each other in the first round in singles, or in doubles if both players on each team are from the same Region, unless there are insufficient entries to do otherwise.

8. In addition to the seeded entries, in the case of only two entries from any one country, they shall be drawn in separate halves of the draw, and not less than the four best entries from one country, but not more than eight, shall be drawn in separate quarters or eighths, as the case may be. Note: Again treat states or regions in the United States as Countries in this matter.

Scoring Systems

The following systems are recommended by the United States Badminton Association as various methods for determining the winning team when two or more schools or clubs compete against each other.

1. DUAL MATCHES (2 SCHOOLS OR CLUBS)
   a. Players play each other according to their ranking on the team and the winner is the team with the most victories. The number of positions to be played must be determined before the team match. (Example: Five Men Singles matches with #1 playing #1, #2 playing #2, etc., Five Women's Singles matches; Two Men's Doubles, Two Women's Doubles and Five mixed doubles. The team which wins 10 or more of the nineteen matches is the winner.
   b. Thomas or Uber Cup Style: Three Singles players and Two Doubles Teams (these numbers can be adjusted to suit the Teams involved). Singles players and/or doubles teams must play each of the opponent's singles players and/or doubles teams. Winning team is the team with the most victories.

Example of Seeded Draw

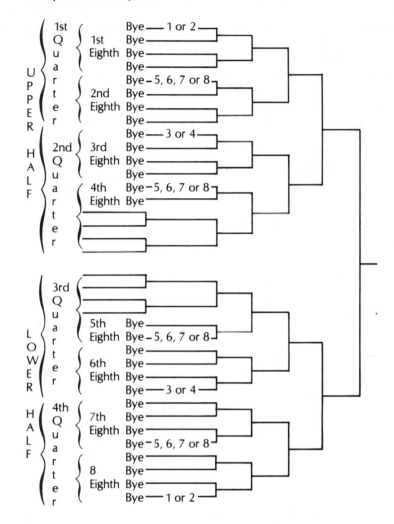

2. Several Teams
   a. Single Elimination Tournament: Unlimited entries from any one team. An attempt should be made that players from the same team should be in different sections of the draw. 2 points are awarded for each match won (if doubles team is from two different teams, split the points.) Player or team receiving a bye will be awarded 4 points if the next match is won or 0 points if the next match is lost. 2 points are awarded for a match won by default. Semi-finalists receive a bonus of 2 points—Finalist receives a bonus of 2 points—Winners receive a bonus of 2 points. If a consolation bracket is played, fractional points should be given in this bracket, but far less than in championships so that players will not intentionally lose to get into this bracket. (Suggest one point for each win in the consolation bracket.)

Team winner is the team with the highest point total.

A single elimination tournament with entries from each team limited to 4 players (each placed in a different quarter of the draw) can be played with the above or similar rules.

b. Round Robin Tournament: Each team enters the same number of singles players and doubles teams. Round-robin tournaments are played in each position (i.e. all #1 players play each other, all #2 players play each other, etc.) Each victory scores one point for the team and high point total is the team winner.

If there are many teams entered, so that the round robin event involves a lot of matches, a single game to 21 may be substituted for a two-out-of-three game match.

Thought Provoker

What would be the ruling for each of the following situations?

1. Player "A" hits the shuttle into opponent player "B." The shuttle hits "B" in the chest and falls to the ground.
   Answer—

2. Player "A" hits a hairpin shot and brushes the net with the body.
   Answer—

3. Player "A" hits the shuttle on his/her side of the net and follows through over the net with the racket after contacting the shuttle.
   Answer—

4. A shuttle is legally served and is allowed to drop by the receiver, it hits the front edge of the correct service line.
   Answer—

5. Player "A" swings at the shuttle and misses it and the shuttle lands outside the court area.
   Answer—

6. The serve is placed and the shuttle hits the top of the net and proceeds to land in the front of the opponent's service box—the receiver allows it to land without touching it.
   Answer—

7. The server puts the shuttlecock into play and the racket head is ¾ of the way beneath the wrist and the shuttle is contacted below waist level.
   Answer—

8. In doubles play, a serve is put into play and goes to the correct box but the receiver's partner in the opposite service box plays the shuttle.
   Answer—

9. In doubles play, a serve is put into play and goes to the incorrect box and the incorrect receiver (in that box) plays the shuttle.
   Answer—

10. A shuttle goes out of bounds on a rally and is hit by the receiver and goes back over the net into the playing area.
    Answer—

Badminton Terminology

Thought Provoker

14

Playing the game of badminton requires skill, strength, speed and intelligence. Another important aspect of badminton is communication. The following glossary of terms provides the participant with the fundamental language of badminton used in the United States.

ABA/USBA   United States Badminton Association. The governing body of badminton in the United States that was founded in Boston in 1936 as the American Badminton Association. The name was changed in 1976.

Alley   The one and one-half foot or .46 meter extension area of the singles court that lies between the singles side line and the doubles side line. Referred to in the United Kingdom as the "tramline."

Attacking Clear   An offensive shot that just clears the overhead reach of the opponent while traveling to the backcourt of the opponent.

Back Alley   The two and one-half foot or .76 meter area that lies between the back boundary line and the long service line for doubles.

Back Court   The rear six feet or 1.82 meters of the court closest to the back boundary line.

Backhand   The side of the court opposite to that of the dominant racket arm. If the racket arm is right, the backhand is to the left side of the player.

Balk   A movement that disconcerts or disturbs the opponent before or during the service. See Law 14d.

Bird   The label given to the shuttlecock or shuttle.

Block   Placing the racket face in a fixed position so that when the shuttle is contacted, it rebounds to the opponent's court without a swinging motion.

Carry   Momentarily holding the shuttle on the racket face during execution of a shot, which is a fault.

Center Court Position   The basic positions that the player assumes in relation to the opponent, court, net and shuttle.

Clear   A high deep shot hit to the back two and one-half feet or .76 meters of the court.

Combination Doubles Formation   A rotating combination of the side-by-side and up-and-back doubles formations.

Court   The official area of play. For singles 44′ x 17′ (13.40m x 5.18m) and for doubles play 44′ x 20′ (13.40m x 6.10m).

Cross Court   A shot whose flight pattern angles diagonally from the point of contact on one side of the court to the other side of the opponent's court.

Deception   Deceiving the opponent by disguising the pace and direction of the shuttle at the very last moment.

Double Hit   The illegal act of contacting the shuttle twice in succession on the same stroke.

Drive   A hard shot whose flight pattern is parallel to the floor while just skimming over the net.

Drive Serve   A hard serve whose flight pattern is parallel to the floor and directed at the receiver's backhand shoulder.

Drop Shot   A shot whose flight pattern finds the shuttle just clearing the net and immediately falling below the level of the net on the opponent's side of the court.

Fault   Any violation of the rules during play.

First Service   A doubles term identifying the player who is the first to serve, implying that the partner has yet to serve.

Flick   Refers to the sudden wrist action required to propel the shuttle faster than the opponent is expecting. It provides a deceptive variant of the low serve and may also be used in the underhand clear.

Foot Fault   An illegal moving or positioning of the feet during service. See Laws 14c and 16.

Forecourt   The six and one-half foot or 1.98 meters area between the net and the short service line.

Forehand   The racket arm side of the court.

Game   A game consists of 15 points for men's singles and all doubles games and 11 points for women's singles. See Law 7.

Game Bird   The point that will enable the serving side to win the game.

Hairpin   A net shot made from below and close to the net. The flight pattern of the shuttle travels straight up, trickles over the net and falls straight down, thus resembling a hairpin.

Half Court Shot   A shot placed to the midcourt area of the opponent. A midcourt drive is an example of such a shot.

IBF   International Badminton Federation. The governing body of badminton for most of the world that was founded in 1934.

Inning   The term of serving for one side.

"In Play"   A shuttle is "In play" from the time struck by the server's racket until it touches the ground or a fault occurs.

"In" Side   The player or team having serving privileges.

Kill   Usually refers to a rally winning smash shot.

Let   A legitimate cessation of play due to any unforeseen or accidental hindrance. The rally may be replayed.

Love   A French term meaning zero.

Love All   A term meaning the score is 0–0.

Match   The best two of three games constitutes a match.

Match Point   The point which, if won by the serving team, terminates the match.

Midcourt   The area of the court from the short singles line to a point six feet or 1.82 meters from the back boundary line.

Net Shot   A shot hit from the forecourt such as the underhand net clear and drop, hairpin, dump and push.

No Shot   A call dictated by etiquette (in the absence of an umpire) indicating that the player has committed a fault by carrying, slinging or throwing the shuttle.

"Out" Side   The player or team receiving the serve.

Overhead   A striking pattern where the point of contact with the shuttle is well above head height.

Passing Shot   A shot that passes to the forehand or backhand side of the opponent.

Pop-Up   A forced defensive "get" resulting in a weak high return.

Push Shot   A shot gently pushed over the net without strong arm action.

Rally   The exchange of the shuttle back and forth over the net.

Ready Position   The "awareness" position that the player assumes when waiting for the opponent to strike the shuttle.

Receiver   The player who accepts the service.

Round-the-Head-Shot   A shot taken with a forehand overhead striking pattern where the point of contact with the shuttle is over the player's backhand shoulder.

Rush-the-Serve   A quick move after the shuttle has been served low by the opponent to intercept the shuttle above the level of the net and put it away.

Second Server   A term used in doubles to indicate that one person on the team has lost the serve.

Serve or Service   The stroke used in putting the shuttle into play.

Service Court   The area of the opponent's court that the shuttle must be delivered to when serving.

Service Over   The umpire's call when service is lost.

Setting   The procedure of extending a game that is tied by increasing the number of points required to win. See Law 7.

Set-Up   A poor shot that invites the opponent to kill or put away the shuttle. Often a shot popped up in the immediate net area.

Shaft   The part of the racket located between the grip and the head.

Shuttlecock   The official name for the bird or shuttle which is usually made from nylon or goose feathers.

Side-by-Side   A doubles formation where one partner plays beside the other and each partner assumes responsibility for half of the court. Primarily used in defense.

Sling or Throw   A term used to indicate an illegal "carry" or holding of the shuttle on the racket face.

Smash   A hard overhead shot angled toward the floor of the opponent.

Stroke   The striking pattern made by the racket as it makes contact with the shuttle.

Toss of Coin or Racket   Procedure to establish the right to select between the options of serving, receiving or defending a particular side.

Underhand   A striking pattern employed when the shuttle is contacted below the level of the net and is too low to employ a side arm or drive shot.

Up-and-back   A doubles and mixed doubles formation where the more powerful partner is responsible for the backcourt area and the remaining partner plays the net area.

Wood Shot   A shot in which the shuttle is hit by part of the frame of the racket rather than the strings or by the frame and strings simultaneously. This shot was legalized in 1963 (see Sling or Throw).

Reconstruct a badminton singles and doubles court. Please label all lines and court areas and identify each court's proper dimensions.

15

Bibliography and Selected Readings
Information and Literature Sources
Audio-Visual Aids
Thought Provoker

Bibliography and Selected Readings

Annarino, A. A., *Badminton Individualized Instructional Program,* Englewood Cliffs, New Jersey: Prentice-Hall, Inc., 1973.

Barrow, H. M., Crisp, M., and J. W. Long, *Physical Education Syllabus,* Minneapolis, Minnesota: Burgess Publishing Company, 1967.

Bergstrom, J. and E. Hultman, Nutrition for Maximal Sports Performance, *Journal of the American Medical Association,* August 23, 1972.

Bloss, M. V., *Badminton,* Dubuque, Iowa: Wm. C. Brown Company Publishers, 1980.

Breen, J. L., and E. Paup, *Badminton,* Chicago, Illinois: The Athletic Institute, 1983.

Brumbach, W. B. and R. B. Ballou, "A brief outline of background material on the sport of badminton," *Physical Educator,* 1963.

Burris, B. J. and A. L. Olson, *Badminton,* Boston, Massachusetts: Allyn and Bacon, Inc., 1974.

Davidson, K. R., "Badminton, Footwork and Body Balance," *Scholastic Coach,* 1950.

Davidson, K. and L. C. Smith, *Badminton,* Chicago, Illinois: The Athletic Institute, 1952.

Davidson, K. R. and L. R. Gustavson, *Winning Badminton,* New York: The Ronald Press Company, 1953.

Davis, P., *The Badminton Coach: A Manual for Coaches, Teachers, and Players.* New Rochelle, New York: Sportshelf, 1976.

E. I. Dupont de Nemours and Co., *Engineering Design,* Wilmington, Delaware: Dupont Company, 1977.

Finston, I. L., and C. Remsberg, *Inside Badminton.* Chicago: Contemporary Books, Inc., 1978.

Fox, K., "Beginning Badminton Examination," *Research Quarterly, 24:*135–146, 1953.

Fox, M. G., and V. P. Young, "Effect of Reminiscence on Learning Selected Badminton Skills," *Research Quarterly, 33:*386–394, 1962.

French, F. L., and E. Statler, "Study Skill Tests in Badminton for College Women," *Research Quarterly, 20:*257–272, 1949.

Gallway, W. T., *Inner Tennis: Playing the Game,* New York: Random House, Inc., 1976.

Gray, C. A. and W. B. Brumbach, "Effect of Daylight Projection of Film Loops on Learning Badminton," *Research Quarterly, 38:*562–569, 1967.

Hatfield, F. C. and M. L. Krotee, *Personalized Weight Training for Fitness and Athletics: From Theory to Practice,* Dubuque, Iowa: Kendall/Hunt Publishing Company, 1978.

Hennis, G., "Badminton Knowledge Test for College Women," *Research Quarterly, 27:*301–309, 1956.

Howard, O. "United States Takes Up Badminton," *The Literary Digest,* October, 1933.

International Badminton Federation, *The International Badminton Federation Statute Book,* Cheltenham, England: International Badminton Federation, 1977.

Jackson, C. H., and L. A. Swan, *Better Badminton,* New York: A. S. Barnes and Company, 1939.

Krotee, M. L. and F. C. Hatfield, "The Theory and Practice of Physical Activity," Dubuque, Iowa: Kendall/Hunt Publishing Company, 1979.

Lifetime Sports Education Project, *Ideas for Badminton Instruction,* Washington, D.C.: American Association of Health, Physical Education and Recreation, 1966.

Lockhart, A. and F. A. McPherson, "The development of a test of badminton playing ability," *Research Quarterly, 20:*402–405, 1949.

McCloy, C. H., "Parlor Badminton," *Journal of Health, Physical Education and Recreation,* 1949.

Millar, F. A., "A Badmintonn Wall Volley Test," *Research Quarterly* 22:208–213, 1951.

National Association of Girls and Women's Sports, "Tennis/Badminton/Squash Guide," (Current Issue) Washington, D.C.: American Alliance for Health, Physical Education and Recreation.

Pelton, B. C., *Badminton,* Englewood Cliffs, New Jersey: Prentice-Hall, Inc., 1971.

Phillips, M., "Standardization of a Badminton Knowledge Test for College Women," *Research Quarterly, 17:*48–63, 1946.

Poole, J., *Badminton,* Glenview, Illinois: Scott, Foresman and Company, 1982.

Rogers, W., *Advanced Badminton,* Duqubue, Iowa: Wm. C. Brown Company Publishers, 1970.

Rutledge, A., "Let's Teach Badminton," *Journal of Health, Physical Education and Recreation,* March, 1955.

Rutledge, A. and J. Friedrich, *Beginning Badminton,* Belmont, California: Wadsworth Publishing Company, Inc., 1969.

Scott, M. G., "Achievement Examinations in Badminton," *Research Quarterly,* 12:242–253, 1941.

Scott, M. G. and E. French, *Measurement and Evaluation in Physical Education,* Dubuque, Iowa: Wm. C. Brown Company Publishers, 1959.

Seaton, D. C., Clayton, I. A., Leibee, H. C., and L. L. Messersmith, *Physical Education Handbook,* Englewood Cliffs, New Jersey: Prentice-Hall, Inc., 1974.

Terauds, J. (ed.), *Science in Racquet Sports.* Delmar, California: Academic Publishers, 1979.

Information and Literature Sources

American Alliance for Health, Physical
  Education, Recreation and Dance
Technique Charts
1900 Association Drive
Reston, Virginia 22091

Badminton Gazette
Badminton Association of England
81a High Street Bromley
Kent, England BR 1 3JU

Badminton Review
The Canadian Badminton Association
333 River Road
Ottawa
Ontario, Canada KlL8B9

Badminton Rules
Dayton Racquet Company
Arcanum, Ohio 45304

Badminton USA
Periodical of the United States Badminton
  Association
Guide to Better Badminton
Ashaway Products Incorporated
Ashaway, Rhode Island 02804

International Badminton Federation
24 Winchcombe House
Cheltenham, Gloucestershire
England GL52 6YB

Racquets Canada
643 Yonge Street
Toronto, Canada

Shuttle Scuttle
c/o Kelly Tibbetts
4431 Pacific Coast Highway
Apt. L–202
Torrance, CA 90505

United States Badminton Association
P.O. Box 237
Swartz Creek, Michigan 48473

Audio-Visual Aids

Advanced Badminton. Wynn Rogers. AIMS Instructional Media Services, Inc., P.O.Box 1010 Hollywood, California 00028.

Assorted Badminton Films. R. Stanton Hales, 1143 Yale Avenue, Claremont, California 91711.

Audio-Visual Film Loops, Lifetime Sports Badminton. AAHPERD Publications, 1900 Association Drive, Reston, Virginia 22091.

Badminton Fundamentals. AIMS Instructional Media Services, P.O. Box 1010, Hollywood, California 90028.

Badminton Loops (16mm). Educational Productions, Inc., 915 Howard Street, San Francisco, California 94103.

Badminton Sports Techniques. Athletic Institute, 805 Merchandise Mart, Chicago, Illinois 60654.

Basic Badminton. Ealing Film Loops, 2225 Massachusetts Avenue, Cambridge, Massachusetts 02140.

Fundamentals of Badminton. All American Productions and Publishers, c/o George B. Pearson, Department of Physical Education, Florida International University, Miami, Florida 33199.

Let's Play Badminton, General Sportcraft Company, Ltd., 33 New Bridge Road, Bergenfield, New Jersey 07612.

1967 All England Championships. Hashman-Takagi Match, J. Frank Devlin, Dolfield Road, Owings Mills, Maryland 21117.

1969 U.S. Nationals Matches. Dr. Charles Thomas, Northwestern State College of Louisiana, Natchitoches, Louisiana 71457.

1971 Canadian Open Finals (16mm) and the *1970 Canada vs. Denmark Match* (16mm). (Separate Audio Tape). Canadian Badminton Association, 333 River Road, Ottawa, Ontario, Canada KIL8B9.

Selected Highlights—1973 U.S. Open Badminton Championships. (Video Tapes) The Travelers Insurance Companies, One Tower Square, Hartford, Connecticut 06115.

Selected Highlights of the 1969 U.S. Open Amateur Championships. David Ogata, 3919 Alla Road, Los Angeles, California 90066.

Thought Provoker

Take an 8″ × 11″ piece of lined or unlined paper and construct an audiovisual aid that you could use to help yourself or another player better understand some aspect of the game of badminton.

Creative Activities for
the Game of Badminton

16

This chapter is an attempt to provide the reader a starting point to enter the world of creative insights of the game of badminton. The activities included in this chapter should be just a beginning for the reader to start his/her own journey into developing new and creative activities for badminton.

Creative Activities

Change the color of the shuttlecock by using spray paint. Try iridescent colors, two tones, and others.

Paint the badminton court different colors. Try different colors in the alley, service court, and forecourt.

Raise and lower nets at different point intervals during the game.

Employ duckbill cardboard blinders with head bands so that the duckbill is below the eyes and the player cannot look down and see the court. This develops court sense and court awareness.

Increase or decrease the playing area. Make the court twice as large or half again as small as a normal sized court.

Alter the shape of the court from a rectangle to a square, circle, oval, diamond, or triangle.

Play mixed siamese twin doubles where a short piece of rope (3' or one meter in length) joins the mixed doubles partners at waist. (Safety should be stressed). Then play the game.

Employ various types of music from popular, jazz and classical items. Play records at fast or slow speeds instead of normal speed.

Invent new strokes that do not now exist, such as between the legs, and around the back shots. Create innovative names for the new strokes.

Modify the regulation game by changing service rules, scoring patterns, and rotation sequences.

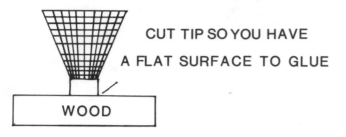

CUT TIP SO YOU HAVE
A FLAT SURFACE TO GLUE

WOOD

4" – 6" square

Figure 16.1. "Silver Shuttle" award construction.

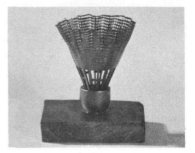

Figure 16.2. The "Silver Shuttle" award.

Employ various relays that are typical to all activities such as run and shoot the basketball until you get it through the hoop—run to the service box and successfully hit a low short serve to a targeted area and then run and tag the next team member. Attempt to keep the shuttle in this targeted area during the relay.

Design board games similar to Scrabble, Monopoly, Parcheesi, concentration, or Tic-tac-toe, and employ badminton terms, rules skills and concepts in these newly developed games. Employ multimedia bombardment techniques to introduce new aspects of badminton.

Use 2 slide projectors, 2—16mm film projects, 2 loop projectors to introduce the serve. Project all on one wall or on different walls, floor and ceiling.

Have in-class tournaments for students using draw sheets with students' names and badminton names such as Betty "Backcourt" Smith or Robert "Round-the-Head" Jones. Present home-made trophies to the various participants such as the "Silver Shuttle", a block of wood with a shuttle glued to it and painted silver (Figures 16.1 and 16.2).

Pivot practice by placing three parallel lines 4' or 1.2 meters apart on the floor. Stand on middle line and pivot and lunge to either of the other two lines, return to the center line and pivot and lunge to the other side. Concentrate on improving your footwork.

Divide court up into sections with a home base—on command move to the section given and mimic proper stroke and then return to home base. For example, area #6 is the high clear area, or area #1 is the hairpin area (Figure 16.3).

Try rotation badminton where two players or four players are on the court. Hit one specific shot and rotate out. Try one racket per team (Figure 16.4).

Make use of sheets strung at different heights above the net depending on shots desired to practice. Holes may be placed in the sheets and then attempt to hit shuttle through the holes or over sheets (Figure 16.5).

Try rallyminton where each player must hit the shuttlecock a given number of times before either player can score.

Play double jeopardy where both players of a doubles team must hit the shuttlecock before it goes over the net or before they can score.

Play a match or practice with two or more shuttle cocks in use at the same time.

Practice drives in a low ceiling with a space about 6' or 2 meters high to improve keeping drives close to top of the net.

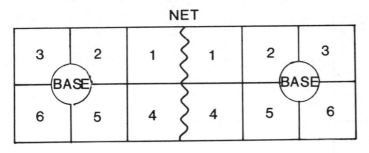

Figure 16.3. Home base badminton.

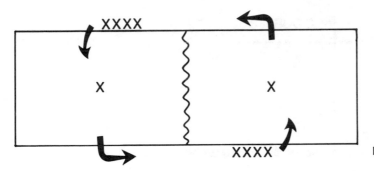

Figure 16.4. Rotation badminton.

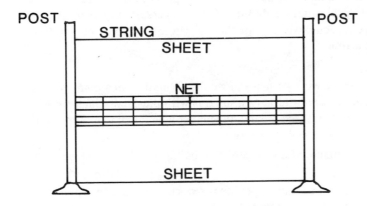

Figure 16.5. Sheet badminton.

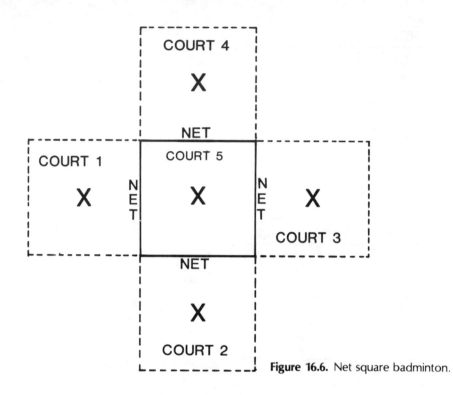

Figure 16.6. Net square badminton.

Play balloonminton where a balloon replaces the shuttlecock.

Replace the net with two ropes and play regular badminton rules except that the shuttlecock must pass between the two ropes. Play 4 net square badminton for 5 players or 10 players (Figure 16.6). Each of the 5 or 10 players (doubles) may hit the shuttle to any court at any time. Employ two or more shuttles at a time.

Play badminton without a net.

Reverse scoring procedure so that low score wins—when you would normally win a point you lose one. Divide court into 3' or 1 meter squares alternating squares with plus and minus numbers in each square. When the shuttle finally hits the ground, the player who failed to hit the shuttle is awarded the point value of square where shuttle hits.

Badminton baseball in a small baseball diamond all rules of baseball apply. Of course no hands are permitted.

Try back line badminton where the players must remain behind the baseline during the game using only high clears and drives. You score if the opponent fails to place the shuttle where you can reach it. Place the line in closer if the baseline is too deep.

Play the game between the net and short service line with only net shots permitted.

Try doubleminton where each player holds a racket in each hand and the game is played.

Figure 16.7. Tic-tac-toe badminton.

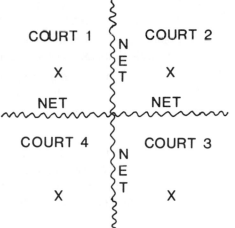

Figure 16.8. Courtminton.

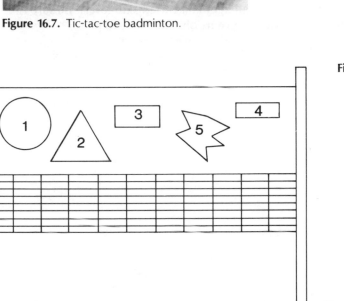

Figure 16.9. Holeminton.

Draw 9 squares over each 1/2 of the court and play Tic-tac-toe by employing various underhand strokes with opponents alternating hits but allowing the shuttle to hit. There are no rallies, X's and O's of paper are then placed appropriately after each shot (Figure 16.7).

Two net—four courtminton where two nets are criss-crossed and 4 courts are formed. The shuttle may be played to any court at any time (Figure 16.8).

Support or hang an innertube so that it can be raised and lowered from the ceiling. Practice hitting various clears by placing them through the tube.

Doubles with one racket per team. Players must share racket and pass it to one another after each successful hit.

Play holeminton where a piece of cardboard (3' or 1 meter high) with net width holes is placed above the net supported by string and standards. Holes of various shapes and sizes are cut through cardboard and each hole is given a point value. The game is played by hitting the shuttle through the cardboard holes and you receive the point value of the hole through which shuttle passes (Figure 16.9).

Try handminton where 4 players play a game of badminton on a 1/4 size court (lower the net) using only their hands to hit the shuttlecock. (No rackets)

Modified point scoring. A point in a regular game may be scored when a certain type of shot is employed. Such as rally but you can only score off a backhand hairpin shot.

Play in a court 4 times the regulation size with 6 team members on a side. Volley the shuttle similar to volleyball. The net is also higher.

Play badminton soccer. Lower the net and kick the shuttle into a confined space. Use volleyball rules.

These are just a few of the creative activities that can be employed to teach the concepts of time, space, flow, power, force and cooperation. These creative activities as well as other modified badminton activities may be employed by players of all ages and varied skill levels. Be sure that safety is always emphasized especially where space and court obstructions are present.

Thought Provoker Answers

APPENDIX

Chapter 1—The following items can be found in the drawing.

China	Thomas Cup
England	Uber Cup
Battledore	USBA
India	5'
Poona	15 Pts.
1895	Racket weight
1878	Shuttlecock
	Racket

Chapter 2—The solution to the crossword puzzle is as follows.

Across
1. Mental
2. Heart rate
3. Muscle
4. Distractions
5. Individual

Down
1. Legwork
2. Weaknesses
1. Psychological
4. Wrist
5. Fatigue

Chapter 3—Matching answers with reasoning.

A. Continental—do not need to change grips during match.
B. Parallel—so you can easily pivot in any direction.
C. Center—you can more easily get to all shots—it is the offensive position.
D. Spread—to give more stability to grip.
E. Side-by-side—they then cover equal areas.
F. Rotation-flexion—moves the racket through a greater range of motion thus more force.
G. Wrist—all sources of power are used but the culminating force comes from wrist snap.
H. Combination side-underhand swing—gives more power then strict underhand.
I. Hits shuttle—gives greatest deception.

Chapter 4—The following fairy tale items relate to badminton:

Feet comfortably apart

Perfectly still

Below her waist

Side-by-side

Up-and-back

Slightly bending her knees and waist

Balls of the feet

Sidearm-underarm action

Upward high and deep

Flicks

Flight

Chapter 5—

Clear 1. The trajectory is much too low and too short. There may be a lack of power—check power sources. The racket face might be too closed caused by playing shuttle too far forward of the body plane. The only positive point is that it cleared the net.

Clear 2. The trajectory is high enough but much too short. It could be a lack of power and/or allowing the shuttle to be played too far behind the body.

Clear 3. There is ample power since the shuttle travels the length of the court. However, the trajectory is too low caused by a closed racket face from playing shuttle too far in front of the body.

Clear 4. This is basically an accurate high deep clear from baseline to baseline.

Clear 5. The shuttle is deep enough in the opponent's court but is not high enough. Very seldom is a clear hit from such a close net position. It would be a good "push" clear if the opponent was caught at the net.

Chapter 6—

1. Sidearm
2. Baseline
3. Parallel
4. Offensive
5. Close
6. Cross court and down the line.

Chapter 7—

1. Down
2. Deception
3. Court
4. Wrist
5. Net
6. High

Chapter 8—

1. Down
2. Hard
3. Lethal
4. Power
5. Front Court
6. Half Smash
7. Offensive
8. High Clear
9. Grunt
10. Forehand

Chapter 9—

The round-the-head shot is a sophisticated technique which is a delivery vehicle to replace the backhand stroke. For the round-the-head shot to be successful, all mechanical aspects of the skill must be fluid. If all aspects of the skill are not performed to their optimum, the round-the-head shot would not be successful.

Chapter 10—

1. As one hits the fly on a fragile object, you must hit with a flick and stop your power before contact or you will break the fragile object. In hitting a net shot you must absorb the power of a shot and employ the wrist flick to control the shuttle.
2. In catching a hard thrown tennis ball, you must control the ball with the hands and give with the initial impact so the hands can control the ball (absorbing the shock). In flicking a net shot off a smash, you must give with the racket in order to control the shuttle and delicately return it over the net.
3. While lifting the heavy object overhead, you must push the object up just as you also must employ a pushing action in certain net shots.
4. Snapping the fingers is a quick decisive action. The reaction needed for hitting many net shots must also be that fast.

Chapter 11—

1. Court sense is basically understanding where you are on the court at all times and where your opponent is and where the opponent plans to move. Court sense also entails proper shot selection to keep the opponent moving and off balance. Court sense is also concerned with court awareness such as knowing if a shuttle is going in bounds or is out of play.

Chapter 12—

1. False. They are made of composite materials including carbon, graphite and fiberglass as well as metal.
2. True. The nylon shuttle is cheaper and more sturdy. Feathered shuttles tend to break easily especially when used by beginners.
3. False. There are many suppliers and companies who provide quality badminton equipment.
4. False. The quality of the net is dictated by its cost. The cheaper cost the cheaper quality the net and vice-versa.
5. False, This is too low. Many shuttles will hit the ceiling. Twenty-four to thirty feet or ten meters clearance would be much better.
6. False. Shorts allow for more freedom of movement which is paramount in the game of badminton.
7. True. No regulations currently exist to govern the size of badminton rackets.
8. False. There are several different weights of shuttles for indoor and outdoor play.

Chapter 13—

1. Player "A" either gains a point or wins service.
2. The striker loses a point or serve. You cannot touch the net with your body.
3. This is legal as long as the shuttle was first contacted on his/her side.
4. This is a good serve and a point is awarded to the server.

5. The swing is incidental as the shuttle is still out and "A" would win a point or service.
6. A point for the server. As long as the serve goes into the correct service court it matters not whether or not it touches the net.
7. This is illegal and results in the loss of serve. The racket head must be totally below the wrist.
8. This is a point for the server. The individual in the correct box must play the shuttle not their partner.
9. A point for the server. If the incorrect receiver had allowed the serve to drop, it would have been a loss of serve.
10. The shuttle is still in play. This was a mistake by the receiver since he/she could have allowed shuttle to hit out of bounds and won a point or service. Since the receiver played the shuttle, it is considered in play.

Chapter 14—Badminton singles and doubles court diagram.

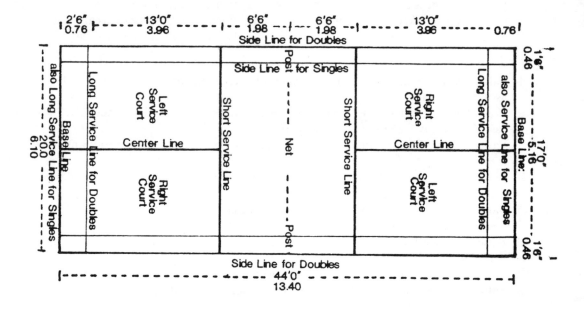

Chapter 15—A few possible creative ideas.

1. Use the paper as targets for the serve.
2. Place key words on a paper regarding a specific skill and post near the court.
3. Roll up into a ball and use to hit instead of a shuttle.
4. Place on the floor as a reminder about some aspect of shot placement.